"Connoisseurs of nature and good writ by his first-person wildlife encounters... clarity, lyrical tilt and a story-teller's skill *BBC Countryfile*, Book of the Month

"All luminous moments, small delights and bright meditations drawn from the northern cold... Crumley invites us to linger a while and witness frosty gifts made vivid by the warmth of his conversation." MIRIAM DARLINGTON, *BBC Wildlife*

"Inviting and informative...Crumley has earned himself the enviable position of our foremost nature commentator... Meditative...bewitching...outspoken...persuasive...a true winter's tale." ROSEMARY GORING, *Herald*

Praise for The Nature of Autumn and previous titles:

LONGLISTED for the **Wainwright Book Prize 2017**

SHORTLISTED for a **Saltire Society Literary Award 2014**

"A delightful meditation." STEPHEN MOSS, *The Guardian*

"Breathtaking ...with characteristic moments of close observation, immersion and poetry ... a delight." *BBC Wildlife*

"A book that quietly celebrates life, at the very moment life is most quietly celebrating itself." *Herald*

"Enchanting." SARA MAITLAND, *BBC Countryfile*

"Crumley conveys the wonder of the natural world at its wildest ...with honesty and passion and, yes, poetry." SUSAN MANSFIELD, *Scottish Review of Books*

"Scotland's pre-eminent nature writer." *Guardian*

"Crumley's distinctive voice carries you with him on his dawn forays and sunset vigils." JOHN LISTER-KAYE, *Herald*

"The best nature writer working in Britain today." DAVID CRAIG, *Los Angeles Times*

"Enthralling and often strident." *Observer*

"Well-written ... elegant. Crumley speaks revealingly of 'theatre-in-the-wild'." *Times Literary Supplement*

Also by Jim Crumley

The
Nature of
Winter

Jim
Crumley

Saraband

Published by Saraband,
Digital World Centre
1 Lowry Plaza, The Quays
Salford, M50 3UB

and

Suite 202, 98 Woodlands Road
Glasgow, G3 6HB

www.saraband.net

ISBN: 9781912235179
ISBNe: 9781912235094

Editor: Craig Hillsley

Printed and bound in Great Britain by Clays Ltd, Elcograf S.p.A.

10 9 8 7 6 5 4 3 2

For George –
one last time –
with profound gratitude

Contents

The White Bird
Passes Through

THE NATURE OF winter is one of simplicities. The wild world is reduced to its barest essentials. It is a self-portrait worked in low light with a limited palette of pastels. Here, for example, is one such portrait.

You might come across it and think at first glance that you had wandered into the motif for a painting by Monet at the height of his Impressionist powers. Three quarters of the composition is given over to a soft-focus screen of trees at dusk, and this sets the tone, establishes the atmosphere. Individual trees are hinted at rather than rendered explicitly, because between the screen of trees and the viewer there is a second screen, flimsy and translucent, but essential to the startling effect of the whole: it is a screen of falling snow. The remaining quarter of this self-portrait of winter – the bottom quarter – is itself divided into three distinct and shallow horizontal bands. There is first a band of tall grass, which meshes raggedly with the lower parts of the trees. It is a pale, straw-coloured band; it speaks as eloquently as the falling snow of winter, and its shade contrasts sharply with the darkening bluey-greeny-grey of the trees. At the very bottom of the portrait is a slim band of water, pale and featureless and colourless, so the setting is defined as the bank of a river or the shore of a lake. And all these bands of colour – trees, grass and water – stretch from edge to edge as far as the eye can see. There is no vertical emphasis in this self-portrait. All is hunkered down and stretched wide and taut as … well, as taut as an artist's canvas.

The falling snow has just begun, and as yet it clings to nothing, and there is no wind, for it falls straight down, yet it is the snow and the subdued light which impart the sense of the season and the hour of the day. Winter, at the very moment you stand before this self-portrait, is battening down in preparation for a long and very cold night.

It may not sound like much of a portrait (for the writer must always come up short when he tries to render the artist's visualisation with his palette of words), but I have not yet told you about the third horizontal band, the one between the grass and the water. Unlike the other horizontals, it stretches only seven-eighths of the way across the composition from left to right, and it is much shallower than the other bands. Yet the viewer's eye homes in on it at once with the certainty of moth to flame, which is of course precisely what the artist intended. It shows, hunched against the cold, a loosely-spaced frieze of forty-four little egrets. A forty-fifth glides in to land just inside the right-hand edge. The whole thing is one of the most moving and enduring images of nature I have ever seen, and I have been carrying it around in my head for thirty years now. I was asked by someone in the audience at a book festival what I was working on, and when I said that it was a book about the nature of winter, she asked,

"And what does that look like?" I said it was still a secret, but what I could have said was, "A long line of forty-four little egrets standing on the shore of a lake at dusk just as the snow starts falling, and a forty-fifth little egret glides in to land."

And it is not a painting by Monet, although the artist has clearly set out to achieve something like an Impressionist effect. In fact, it is not a painting at all, but a photograph. It lies on my oak table as I write, and even on a spring day of bright sunshine it contrives to thrill and chill me in the same instant, as it did that day in 1988 when for the first time I turned a page in one of the most remarkable and downright exquisite nature books I have ever owned, and there it was, and I probably gasped out loud. The book is *The White Egret* (Blandford, 1988) by a Japanese photographer, Shingi Itoh, and time without number in the intervening years I have taken it down from my bookshelves when I felt fed up or ill at ease or dissatisfied with something I had just written, and I have felt my mood lighten or my sense of perspective readjust to a more even keel in the reflected light of its quite magical aura.

Sometimes when I'm out and alone in the company of nature and the raw beauty of the setting takes over from whatever original purpose had led me there, I think about the elusive nature of what I aspire to as a writer, of the arrogance that underpins the ambition to incarcerate what lies before me within the covers of a book. Then I think of Shingi Itoh and his book, and I reassure myself of the merits of the endeavour, if you put in the work, if you approach it in the right frame of mind. In his preface to what is primarily a photographic essay, he wrote:

I have taken more than one hundred thousand photographs of egrets ... the task of capturing the true beauty of the lustrous, snow-white egret on film has been completely beyond my capabilities, although I have continued to take pictures of them. As difficult as this task might be ... I have felt a need to understand the egret's movements and behaviour, their enduring existence, and to share what I have learned ...

One hundred thousand photographs! And one of these, shot at a pre-roosting gathering of little egrets – in what I imagine were agonising winter conditions for wildlife photography – travelled halfway round the world and fell into my hands by happy accident, and made an unlikely disciple in Scotland of the culture of white egrets (in Japan, the bird is a recurring motif in painting, literature, haiku, song and place names). Thank you, Shingi Itoh, for your work and for your sharing; it is a job very well done.

About the time that *The White Egret* was published in Britain, a recovering egret population in France had begun to send emissaries across the English Channel, where they established a pioneering presence along the south coast. The first British breeding record was in Dorset in 1996 and there are now around 700 pairs with more than 4,000 wintering birds. The slow drift northward continues, and solitary travellers have begun to turn up on some unlikely wetlands. For example:

Loch Leven, on the border between Kinross and Fife, January 2017, the day sunny and hazy, the RSPB's Vane Farm reserve drenched by a ragged, undisciplined choir of around

200 curlew voices, a gathering rare enough to be thrilling. It is also begs symbolic questions of where our country stands in its relationship with nature. Curlew fortunes are in steep decline right across Britain, numbers have fallen by two-thirds since 1970, and given that Britain hosts more than a quarter of the world's population, the bird has become a high priority for nature conservation. It is a victim of land use change in particular, the tendency towards commercial forestry and field drainage, the consequent loss of wetlands. In the short term, reserves like this are priceless, for the land is tailored to a perfect habitat for curlews and other troubled species, and it allows people to witness spectacles like this one at close quarters, so that they can watch and listen to nature making its own arguments. Such circumstances create the opportunity for people to see what can be done, and to win new friends for nature's cause. It is essential work.

The curlews moved in from the fields in a constant left-to-right drift low across open water, beyond which was a wide grassy mound where geese grazed. Many of the curlew banked round the far side of the mound and came back over its wide crown in a still-winged glide to the shore. As each bird landed it raised its wings before it settled, a heraldic pose of beauty and balletic poise.

Then one more wave of about thirty curlews came over the mound from the north, and right in the middle of them was a vivid white bird that blazed in the sunlight, and I shook my head in disbelief. Then as the curlews' wings stopped beating and they began to glide, the white bird stretched out a long neck, which I now realised had been tucked inside its shoulders, and I remembered something:

*To maintain balance, the egret untucks its neck when taking
off and landing.*

It was the word "untucks" that had stuck in my mind when
I read the line in Shingi Itoh's book, and I had smiled at the
idea of being able to untuck your neck, like pulling your
shirt out of your trousers. And here, after all these years of
turning the pages of that book with a kind of reverence,
here was a wild white egret not twenty-five miles from my
doorstep. And of course the next thing that came into my
mind was *that* photograph, which so summarised winter for
me by reducing it to its essential simplicities.

It landed, not with the curlews, but alone and on a different
shore, and in the instant of landing it re-tucked its neck. It
walked a few yards, a snow bird on black heron-legs, and
sought the lee of a small clump of tall, reedy grass and began
to preen. At a distance of around a hundred yards, it looked
like a flapping curtain in the wind, until it reassembled itself
and became egret again. Then it ran a few steps, untucked its
neck and flew down a watery channel and just above its own
reflection. I took one photograph, which I will keep until I
get a better one. It is over-exposed and out of focus, neither
of which was surprising in the circumstances, but the pose
is one that is familiar to me. The angle is different, but the
attitude of the bird so low over water is uncannily like the
forty-fifth little egret in Shingi Itoh's photograph, the one
flying into the picture from the right-hand edge.

In my own photograph, the wings extend in a straight
horizontal line from the head to the "elbow" of each wing,

then angle down at about 120 degrees. It is a three-quarters view, so I can see most of the underside of the left wing and, because of a complete fluke of the light, the shadow of the bird's long, black bill is thrown onto the inside of that wing. One photograph – 99,999 fewer than the Japanese maestro – but it was my only souvenir of the moment when the white bird passed through my life (until I wrote this chapter).

I was back at the loch in early April and asked about the egret. The RSPB records revealed that there had been long gaps between sightings on the reserve, but that it had been back just three days before.

In its natural homelands (and, for the moment at least, Scotland is a long way from being one of those) it is a bird that lives in flocks. So why was this single bird so far from other egrets? Where did it come from and how did it get here? And then there is the more troubling question: was its presence here so far north of what I imagine is its comfort zone, and on what was by any standards an unseasonably mild January day, a small but beautifully formed symptom of our warming world, of climate change? Whatever the explanation, I am full of gratitude that our paths crossed and that it let in a little exotic light on my own idea of the nature of winter.

Chapter One

White Walls Weeping

WINTER IS THE ANVIL on which nature hammers out next spring. Its furnace is cold fire. It fashions motes of life. These endure. Even in the utmost extremes of landscape and weather, they endure.

Three thousand feet up in the Cairngorms, and deep in the nadir of the wild year, there is danger of a kind in simply being so exposed to the adrenalin of solitude and silence and the primitiveness of midwinter at its zenith. Strange how the season's zenith and nadir can co-exist in the same place at the same moment.

There is a brink somewhere just ahead. It is not a thing of the landscape, not a cliff edge or a *bergschrund*. It is a thing of the mind. Can you stretch the day's boundaries just a little more? And how much is a little more? How much of this rarefied distillation of solitude can you handle? What do you stand to gain? What do you stand to lose? Look around at the nothing that surrounds you, a nothing saturated in Arctic quantities of snow; surely such nothing-ness is inimical to life?

But a moment ago, a tiny scatter of movement caught my eye and vanished. I stopped in my tracks, literally in my tracks. There were no other tracks. All I could see was white walls weeping, the white walls of an amphitheatre of snow. Snow in billowing downdraughts, snow so solid you could build it into buttresses, snow so fozy and gauzy it hung on the air like curtains of iced steam. I remember thinking perhaps it should be colder at the winter solstice this high on loveable old Bràigh Riabhach. This is my sacred ground. Here in all the tormented, tumultuous geology of the mountain massif we call the Cairngorms is a piece of such singularly dishevelled ground that some unknown someone some unknown sometime ago christened it (with surely malicious understatement) "rough".

An Garbh Choire, the Rough Corrie.

Somewhere down below, down in the belly of the snow cloud that had squatted on these mountains for a week, was the boulderfield of the Làirig Ghrù, a place of underfoot treacheries at the best of times, and this, you could be excused for thinking, was not one of those. Not unless this is your idea of sacred ground; not unless, over the last forty years, this of all mountains has occasionally commanded you to stillness in its company and revealed to you one of its many secrets, leaving you spellbound and speechless; not unless it has mostly done so in winter and mostly when you have been alone; and not unless you are a nature writer for whom such a moment is the living, breathing definition of the Holy Grail.

Somewhere up above, up on the mile-wide summit plateau of Bràigh Riabhach, is where the River Dee liberates itself from the underworld of the mountain's dark red innards into the snow-lit overworld in a single convulsive shiver; and where, when the mood takes them, winter winds shudder and wail at 150 miles an hour.

Between these two fundamental phenomena of this most fundamental of lands is the corrie someone decided to call "rough". In that company it's some accolade. And something fleeting had just caught my eye, and I looked up towards the headwall and all I could see was white walls weeping. And the more I stared, the more I began to wonder if I had seen anything at all. So I stared harder, but the whole corrie was hung with unfathomable layers of snow. The headwall was curtained by teeming downdraughts, lavishly hung folds of falling spindrift. But from time to time, gaps in the curtain briefly opened and these showed momentary glimpses of the snow behind the curtain, snow that clung to the raw stuff of the mountain in blue-grey depths, the pelage of the hoary old remnants of Scotland's Arctic. That further-back snow had plastered the Rough Corrie worryingly smooth. It looked like far too much snow to cling for very long to something so vertical as the corrie headwall.

Choire Bhrotain, the enigmatically named Porridge Corrie, was missing. The glacier that had dragged its creaking, growling carcase this way 10,000 years ago, give or take a millennium, howked out the Porridge Corrie *en passant*, an oh-what-the-hell-why-not whim, and made a corrie within a corrie there, a gratuitous roughening up of the Rough Corrie, an extra helping of *garbh*, a pinch of rock salt rubbed into the glacial wound. I knew it was there because I have often seen it before, explored its edges in less onerous seasons than this. I knew where it hung, like a picture of a corrie on a corrie wall, high up there on my right, because I was standing by the young Dee and I was facing upstream, and as long as I kept the river in my sight, the map of the corrie in my head would place its component parts on their correct compass points. Roughly.

My stance was a few hundred feet above the Làirig Ghrù, also roughly. I didn't count my footfalls or time my climb. It could be 300 or 400 feet – there are a thousand to play with here between the floor and the rim of the corrie, all of them rough, and mostly I could not see more than about fifty of them at any one time. Even when those gaps opened in the tumbling spindrift, they revealed no known reference points above or below to give them meaning. There was only the river to rely on. I had reassured myself earlier that if conditions should become too much for me (too much flimsy snow, too much mountain, too much Arctic, too much dreich), I would turn and follow it back down to the Làirig, and where it turns right for Aberdeen I would turn left for Coylumbridge. I would refine the process as I walked, but that was the gist.

Then I had started to ask myself if I should be there in such conditions, the familiar self-scrutiny of the solitary mountain wanderer. I had no intention of climbing the corrie walls to the plateau, not with the mountain happed in a fleece as thick as a polar bear's. I became the focal point of a quarrel between two truths. The first truth was that for the sake of my own safety I had no business being there. But the second truth was that I had put myself there because being there is exactly my business. I am more in the business of savouring mountains than climbing them. I do climb them, of course, but with a wanderer's gait rather than a mountaineer's. I don't much like beaten paths or recommended routes, I don't put ticks on lists of summits and I'm no rock climber. I don't frontpoint up frozen waterfalls. I never learned to trust a rope, far less another climber urging me to trust *his* rope. Here, in the Garbh Choire, the river was my rope. Trust that. Climb when you're ready.

And my business is to admire and applaud and marvel at this theatre of the wild, to question it, rather than to participate in it. I am not interested in measuring myself against it, but rather the height of my ambition is to taste it and to write it down. There you are, there is the honesty of my situation: I want to know all this to write it down. If I simply know about it and do nothing with the knowledge then I have no means of articulating my response to it, and responding to the wildest gestures of the nature of my native heath is the best reason I can think of for exploring it. I am a nature writer at heart, this is nature writing on the edge, and I like edges.

The cautionary voice, then, had been silenced by the edginess of the hour, and I had pushed on for the heart of the corrie. Far below and hours ago, considering the day as it dawned from the side of the road at Coylumbridge, a single thought: I wonder how the Garbh Choire looks and feels in this? So here I was finding out, jumaring up the fixed rope of the Dee, and all I could see was white walls, weeping. And all I could hear was the muffled river and the wind that dived down from the plateau and billowed the curtains drawn around the corrie wall. And then something moved that wasn't me and wasn't snow.

I found a rock where the wind was less boisterous, flattened a level shelf in the snow and sat on it. I like being still when nature is in a berserk mood. I like thinking about the natural forces at work on such a mountain on such a day when I am in a position to witness them at work. Being still assists that process.

Almost instantly, I saw spiders. They were tiny and red and they were moving on the surface of the snow, and being still had brought them into focus. They will have a name, these mountaineers for whom one of my footprints is an abyss. Biology will have considered them, mapped them, classified them and given them a Latin name. There was a curious comfort in the presence of another living creature with a purpose in the Rough Corrie that day, even a tiny red spider. I wonder if the Latin-name-giver paused long enough to ponder their purpose. I can only imagine they were hunting, but what the size and nature of their prey might be is beyond my imagining.

And where did they live?

And did they feel the cold?

But it was not little red spiders that had stopped me in my tracks, or made me sit on the mountain. I began to scrutinise the snow for focal points, tried to assess distance, looked for changes in the contours of the visible land where whatever I had seen might take cover or feed or draw breath.

And now I was in my element, in that state of mind which is unknown to the climber who insists on climbing in company. I tasted the thrill of it in the back of my throat. The heightened absorption in my surroundings, the single-mindedness of the job in hand, became the summit of my mountain day. Life rarely gets this simple. I was sitting on a mountainside where nature's mood pushed me to the extreme edge of what I had any right to handle on my own, but it was precisely because I was on my own that I could handle it, and that I could work at this pitch of profound concentration. And then fifty yards away I saw the inch-wide head of a bird move in the snow. I had my focal point, I unsheathed the binoculars, and I found a snow bunting.

Snow buntings are simply among my favourite things. Small squads of them live up here all year round, and not much of anything does that (spiders maybe). A handful of pairs breed on the summits of the land – the Cairngorms and the Ben Nevis group, where the terrain resembles their Icelandic origins – and on bare Shetland tracts. The numbers are guesswork but maybe fifty pairs all told. But migrating thousands flock to our coasts and stubble fields to while away the winter, and there are few more agreeable spectacles on a drab midwinter day than several hundred snow buntings in a loose flock, freewheeling over the machair of the west or the red sandstone clifftops of the east, thickening strands of fence wire to rest between feeding forays. And I once met a solitary brilliant white and glossy black male bird on St Kilda in early June, presumably a late migrant en route home to Iceland. John Love notes in his book, *A Natural History of St Kilda* (Birlinn, 2009), that the snow bunting has only been recorded once as a breeding bird there, and that was in 1913. He also compares St Kilda's origins to Surtsey, the island which rose out of the sea off Iceland in a volcanic convulsion in 1963, then he writes that the first bird to breed on Surtsey was the snow bunting. It is the sheer daring of the bird that delights me.

And now the unblinking black eye of one more male bird was watching me; a scrap of living, breathing warm-blooded-ness at ease in the midst of that most demanding of landscapes in its most demanding winter demeanour. All I could see was the dull brown skull cap, the pale yellow beak, the black eye set in the off-white face, and a pale shadow behind and beneath the eye – for the bird has none of its midsummer splendour in midwinter. Ah, but then it bounced over a tiny rise into full view, and then so did twenty more, and as they bounced they stabbed at the snow, and as the distance between us closed I could see what it was they were eating: red spiders.

And then they flew in that loose-knit make-up of the flock, curved past me, rose twenty or thirty feet and landed again no more than twenty yards away, and as they flew, the snow-white of their wing flashes was a tribal badge, and they chatted in single down-curving notes. And they began again, scouring the snow for its tiny bounties, while the Garbh Corrie rose immensely above and around them, and all its white walls wept.

Suddenly the corrie filled with cloud, a cloud that seemed to consume daylight as it moved. I turned to assess my situation above and behind and below, and when I turned back to the birds they had gone. I stashed the binoculars, shouldered my pack and began to descend the lifeline of the river. Nature had stopped me in my tracks, and now it turned me in my tracks.

For an unbroken hour I walked down through grey-white silence, slipped into what I think of as a hand-in-glove relationship with the mountain, in which there are no distractions and no view, and no company other than the mountain itself, so that you feel the vastness of the massif gathered beneath your feet and reaching down into unimaginable depths below the very curved skin of the planet. You become aware of yourself almost as a creature you can observe from afar and moving minutely across that curving planetary skin, and of no more account in the mountain's scheme of things than a red spider or a snow bunting – less, because they are at home on the mountain whatever its mood, and you, you are a fleeting presence for a few hours, a few days at best.

The scale of the Cairngorms makes these demands on you, and demands of you the quiet patience of the unbroken hours. Then I felt the cloud stir. I stopped and looked around.

There were holes in the cloud below me, and through one of the holes the darkness of trees. There were holes above too, and through one of these a patch of blue that was roughly the shape of the Isle of Mull. And then, over one more afternoon hour, the Cairngorms shed their hodden grey rags to emerge in sunlight as new-born as an adder in its new skin.

There was a sepulchral stillness to the pinewoods in the late afternoon, and all that crossed my path was a treecreeper and a roebuck. The pinewoods passed me on, tree-to-tree, my safe passage down through the dusk. I love the deep green pungency of these trees as I love few other facets of my native landscape. In the Cairngorms they lift you up until they part and offer you the unclothed mountains beyond their outermost shadows, then they reclaim you in the dusk and you feel reabsorbed into an ancient brotherhood of Nature, and I know of nothing else that treats you that way.

Late in the evening I sat in a bar with a fire, a whisky and a full stomach, and I wrote down the head of the snow bunting that emerged from behind an inches-high contour in the snow, and I raised my glass to the black eye at its centre. Up there at midnight, it was as cold as the Icelandic ice cap, but a small flock of snow buntings tholed the long darkness somehow and without fuss, and in the morning there would be more spiders.

There is a school of thought, and it is underpinned by a great deal of convincing science, that if climate change persists on its warming curve, it will remove birds like the snow bunting from our landscapes. If that happens, I might have to move to Iceland.

⊙ ⊙ ⊙

So what's this? I take two steps along my pilgrimage through winter, and each one stumbles over an obstacle on the path, an obstacle that manifests itself not as a protruding stone or an exposed root, not as something I can step over and march on unperturbed, but rather (it seems to me) a thing of dark moods and hidden depths. For the truth is that these two powerful savours of what we like to think of as an idealised winter…the egrets in their blizzard, and the snow buntings in their high mountain world of winter at its most adversarial… these are souvenirs of old winters, and in the second decade of the 21st century such moments have become the exception rather than the rule. Winter is in the throes of becoming something other: something less wintry, something much less predictable, and something infinitely more adversarial, not just for snow buntings and solitary nature writers, but for all of us, for the very well-being of the planet.

Taken in isolation, they may look like inconsequential events, but as I wandered through what winter has become in the course of writing this book, I found myself confronting a single question again and again and again:

Whatever happened to Bleak Midwinter?

Chapter Two

Whatever Happened to Bleak Midwinter?

In the bleak midwinter,
Frosty wind made moan,
Earth stood hard as iron,
Water like a stone;
Snow had fallen, snow on snow,
Snow on snow,
In the bleak midwinter,
Long ago.

CHRISTINA GEORGINA ROSSETTI's 19th-century verse displays a poetic verve a cut above the humdrum hymn-cum-carol in the Church Hymnary. Poetry was her day job after all, and she was one of her century's finest. After that first verse, Hymn 50, as the Kirk has come to think of it, descends into standard Christmas story fare, but that first verse is winter in a nutshell. In particular, I love *Snow had fallen, snow on snow, / Snow on snow.* The word "snow" used five times in two lines – there's a poet's daring for you! The word I have a problem with is "bleak". Lyrically it's perfect, of course, but such a fusion of ice (*Earth stood hard as iron, / Water like a stone*) and relentless snow is the stuff of wonder and beauty, of nature at its utmost. The unwritten next verse should have been the one that reassures: soon the snow would stop, the sun would explode across that snow-on-snow landscape, and diamond dust would drift through village streets so that children would laugh and dance at the miracle of it, and neighbours would come out of their houses and stand in front of their doors, pointing and smiling, cheered and invigorated and enraptured. But which of us can remember the last time that happened? Whatever happened to "bleak" midwinter?

When I wrote this book's predecessor, *The Nature of Autumn* (Saraband, 2016), the full-flavoured technicolour autumn of 2015 that provided much of my research (with adventures from older autumns folded into the mix) was long and lingering and lovely and more or less perfect. The even more lingering autumn of 2016 greatly assisted the book's cause when it was published. It had always been a one-off book in my mind, but when wiser counsel prevailed and it became the first of a quartet of the seasons, it seemed reasonable to me that *The Nature of Autumn* could serve as a kind of template for all four books. I was soon disabused of that idea, for the winter of 2016–17 began as a kind of treacly goo, followed by what the Met Office called "a spell of anti-cyclonic gloom", making it sound more like a troublesome mental condition than a weather forecast. I quickly realised that I was dealing with a very different beast from my autumn book; perhaps even an endangered one, the Scottish wildcat of the seasons, hybridising before my very eyes into something I barely recognised. Even the terminology we have all slipped into – "climate change", "global warming"

– started to jar with me. What is unfolding is climate chaos.

You could argue that the rise and fall of our idea of winter began with the Little Ice Age, which tormented the northern hemisphere between the early 15th and the mid-19th centuries. It first manifested itself as the spread of pack ice and storm in the far North Atlantic. We know that Norse colonies in Greenland were cut off from the influence of their masters on the European mainland, that the west of Greenland succumbed to starvation and an eastern colony was abandoned. Iceland was likewise cut off when sea ice started to surround it entirely every year, and for longer and longer each time. Over the course of the Little Ice Age, the average annual duration of that sea ice cover grew from none at all to forty weeks. All across the northern hemisphere, glaciers extended their reach.

But Greenland was the beginning of it all. In *The Nature of Autumn*, I wrote about a day when I had sensed a troubling restlessness in the land itself in the midst of my own nature-writing territory, of how I tried to listen to it. I have never believed that the land is neutral. I do think it reaches out to us, offering guidance; I do think it is accessible to us if only we are willing to re-learn the lost art of listening to it. That day, I made a long silence for myself at the foot of my local mountain, the result of which was a sense of distress in the landscape that felt like a part of something much larger than the physical confines of what I could see, a sense that nature itself was veering towards a fundamental watershed. That very same evening, I heard for the first time about the potentially catastrophic change in the behaviour of a huge glacier called Zachariae Isstrom. It lies in northmost

Greenland, also known as the cradle of the Little Ice Age, and climate scientists had just announced that it is melting at the rate of five billion tons a year.

◎ ◎ ◎

One hundred years after the end of the Little Ice Age, winter was still reliably supplying nature writers in both Scotland and North America with notably wintry conditions to write about. The Little Ice Age may have slipped below the horizon of living memory, but Bleak Midwinter was still alive and well. This was Seton Gordon, the founding father of all modern Scottish nature writing, in the introduction to his book, *Afoot in Wild Places* (Cassell, 1937):

Winters on islands washed by western seas are always a time of hardship, and the past winter (1936–7) saw more violent and frequent storms than any within living memory. The fishermen suffered many hard blows. Scores of boats were lost or were smashed to pieces at their moorings by the violence of the waves, and many thousands of lobster creels, as well as herring nets and long lines, disappeared in the heavy seas. This disastrous winter, when the earnings of fishing crews were not sufficient to pay for the loss of gear, has caused more men reluctantly to leave their homes and to seek their fortunes elsewhere, and thus another step in the depopulation of the Isles by the younger generation has been taken.

Ten years later, on the other side of the Atlantic, an ecologist called Aldo Leopold was putting the finishing touches to a book which remains the unsurpassed pinnacle of nature writing the world over: *A Sand County Almanac* (Oxford University Press, 1949). It begins in January:

Each year, after the midwinter blizzards, there comes a night of thaw when the tinkle of dripping water is heard in the land. It brings strange stirrings, not only to creatures abed for the night, but to some who have been asleep for the winter. The hibernating skunk, curled up in his deep den, uncurls himself and ventures forth to prowl the wet world, dragging his belly in the snow. His track marks one of the earliest datable events in that cycle of beginnings and ceasings which we call a year.

The track is likely to display an indifference to mundane affairs uncommon at other seasons; it leads straight across-country, as if its maker had hitched his wagon to a star and dropped the reins. I follow, curious to deduce his state of mind and appetite, and destination if any … January observation can be almost as simple and peaceful as snow, and almost as continuous as cold. There is time not only to see who has done what, but to speculate why.

About the time Leopold was immortalising the skunk's emergence, I had decided to emerge myself. I did not actually witness the winter of 1947, although you might say that I was alive and kicking. But it was the July of that year before I eased myself into the world, all 10lbs 3oz of me. My mother – whose first-born, my brother Vic, was only fourteen months old at that point – told me (once I was old enough not to be overly offended): "When I knew I was expecting you, I nearly drowned myself." Happily for all concerned, the notion passed and ours was a family upbringing from which I have harvested only the sweetest of memories. No child of my fresh-air-craving persuasions could have asked for better.

The thing about the winter of 1947 was that it quickly became the stuff of folklore due to the sheer volume of snow that fell between late January and mid-March. Throughout my childhood years, my grandfather often related its events in vivid words. But my grandfather was a storyteller of distinction, and whether he was inventing some off-the-cuff adventure of the Amazonian jungle to entertain his grandsons, or reliving the events of his own lifetime, he was never less than enthralling. So when he pronounced that the year I was born, the winter snows had been piled up in the streets of Dundee as high as the upper decks of the trams and buses, I had trouble imagining what that might look like, and trouble trying to decide whether to believe him. I have since seen the photographs and read the newspaper cuttings, and oh, 'tis true, 'tis true. There had been six weeks of snow, and in Scotland the final assault was the heaviest, and it drifted to a depth of twenty-five feet. Then abruptly, the temperature climbed, the snow melted, but because the land was still frozen, the flooding that followed was equally epic.

The other winter of legend in my own lifetime was 1963, which some sources claim was the coldest for 200 years. But the characteristic of the winters of my young life was that they were reliably wintry. There *would* be snow, there *would* be sledging and snowmen and snowball fights in the school playground, and lo, to some extent or another, Bleak Midwinters came to pass.

But the 21st century has borne witness to a more or less

relentless march towards the decline and fall of winter, with every now and then a brief throwback to remind us of what has gone, and to fill the media with dire headlines forecasting the worst winter since 1963/47, forecasts which never bear fruit. In 2010, the temperature at Altnaharra in Sutherland fell to minus twenty degrees Celsius, which permitted natives of a certain age to tell stories of 1955 when it had reached minus twenty-seven. I liked the much-quoted words of the hotel owner at Altnaharra that winter of 2010: "It's a little bit of winter heaven when the freezing fog lifts. It's really beautiful just now and the scenery is just fantastic."

Alas, she had no hotel guests to share it.

It all depends on the school of thought you inhabit: snow was falling, snow on snow, snow on snow, in the bleak midwinter, long ago ...or a little bit of winter heaven. If only Christina Georgina Rossetti had been marooned in Altnaharra rather than Highgate Hill she might have been of the "little bit of winter heaven" persuasion. After all, it's a better line for a Christmas carol than "In the bleak midwinter".

The nature of winter is transformed and it goes on transforming, in Scotland and around the world. In March of 2017, the World Meteorological Organisation of the United Nations produced its report for 2016. It recorded unprecedented heat across the globe, exceptionally low ice at both poles, rising sea levels, Arctic ice "tracking at record low conditions since October, persisting for six consecutive months", and in the southern hemisphere the least amount of sea ice ever recorded. The WMO also warned that with carbon dioxide in the atmosphere consistently breaking new records, the influence of human activities on the climate system has become more and more evident. It added that "as weather, climate and the water cycle know no national boundaries, international cooperation on a global scale is essential ..."

But alas for international cooperation, a few days earlier the new President of the United States had produced his first budget, which included a thirty-one per cent cut in funding for the Environmental Protection Agency. His spokesman confirmed that the administration would no longer fund measures to combat climate change, adding: "We're not spending money on that any more. We consider that to be a waste of your money."

The leader of the free world had just made a pact with the devil.

☉ ☉ ☉

Yet one of the fascinations of writing a book like this – a series of books like this – is that even as I do my research, compose my arguments and test them against the accumulated fruits of all that I have derived from a life largely spent in nature's company ... even then, the very capriciousness of nature that has so endeared itself to me again and again forever, suddenly drops a pearl in my lap. Perhaps, this particular pearl is telling me, winter is not completely done yet, winter has not yet been completely wiped off the map of the seasons.

Chapter Three

Sweet Medwin Water

THE MAP IN MY hands was published fifty years ago and 300
years after the event that lured me here. It is Bartholomew's
"one inch and a half to the mile" map of the Pentland Hills
and Edinburgh District. There is an old handwritten inscription on its cover in black ink block capitals, which was its
writer's idiosyncratic way with treasured quotations. Even
now, I read the inscription with a shiver of an emotion somewhere between recognition, gratitude and regret, for that
hand was responsible for what must have been hundreds of
letters, postcards, drafts of poems and captions for an endless
stream of cartoons, all of which came my way. And drawings,
of course, always drawings. What the inscription says is this:

> "THE SWEET MONOTONY WHEN
> EVERYTHING IS KNOWN, AND
> LOVED BECAUSE IT IS KNOWN"
> — GEORGE ELIOT

The map is frayed round the edges and broken at all its
corners. The front is so stained on its margins and faded in
the middle that it is now impossible to tell whether it was

originally white (in which case that was surely as stupid a colour for a walker's map as cartographic mankind ever devised) and now tending towards sepia, or the other way round. When you open it out, you find that a large part of the map – the part occupied by the Pentland Hills – has been covered (not by Mr Bartholomew) in overlapping sheets of some kind of clear laminate, and that outwith that area, some of the more weathered folds have been belatedly sellotaped. There are also holes where the tape has succumbed. There are rainwater stains, sleet stains and snow stains, tea stains and coffee stains; and whisky stains for which I was responsible while trying to unite the contents of a hip flask with just the right proportion of sweet Medwin Water one old and dark December day. There are countless other indeterminate stains, the result of decades of manhandling in all winds, all weathers, all seasons. Other than that, it is in pretty good condition, considering the life it has led.

Strictly speaking, this unlovely document is not mine, and it was never in my possession until its rightful owner handed it to me about twenty years ago, having reached that point in his life when he judged that he could make no further use of it. Thinking about it now, the significance of the gift begins suddenly to deepen, and I have never stopped thinking of it as his, as if he might one day materialise out of a thinning mist on a shoulder of Black Law and ask if he might reclaim the map he had lent me. It is just an old worn map of the Pentland Hills, but old worn maps amount to rather more than the sum of their taped-up parts, for they are the unwritten anthologies of the hill days of perhaps half a lifetime. For the better part of the last thirty years of that lifetime, the map's owner was the closest friend I ever knew. His name was George Garson and he was a shipwright-turned-artist (and there are not many of those), whose change of career so prospered that he became a senior lecturer at Glasgow School of Art, a mosaicist and stained glass artist with an international reputation. The Pentland Hills was his soul country, Dunsyre Hill was his Dunadd, and the Medwin Water was his *aqua vitae*.

The Pentlands coursed through all his lives – Edinburgh youth, National Service drill sergeant ("I used to like to make patterns with the marching men!"), shipwright at Henry Robb's yards in Leith and Burntisland, mature student (he went to art college at the age of thirty after a neighbour saw him in the National Gallery of Scotland in Edinburgh when he should have been at work and told Jean, his wife; she confronted him, it turned out it was far from the first time, then told him that if he was going to do art he should do it properly and go to college, and she took on extra work to help him through it), then professional artist, then latterly journalist, poet and author. His art was blessed by the fact that he had built ships, his journalism by the eloquence of his art, his poetry by the unashamedly working-class rootedness of his journalism.

He came from an endless line of Orcadian Garsons and he told me with some pride that the name means "son of the dyke-end". Orkney's horizontally-striated bedrock, and the way the islanders worked with stone, was the seed from which his unique mosaics blossomed. He used slate to mimic the horizontally-stacked stones of Orcadian walls, as consummated in the exquisite 5,000-year-old Maeshowe;

and, inspired by these and the standing stones of such as Brodgar and Stenness, he fashioned a one-man art form. Its finest example, Black Sun of Winter, is in the collection of the Royal Museum of Scotland in Edinburgh. Two smaller slate mosaics hang on a wall of my house, as do drawings, paintings and pastels; and a first-year student piece of wood carving stands on a bookcase. He painted and drew more or less every day until a few days before his death in February 2011, just short of his 80th birthday and less than two years after the death of his beloved Jean.

Orkney was yin to his Pentlands yang. The words "I'm a Garson" were a mantra that opened many doors to him in Orkney, not least his long friendship with George Mackay Brown (and it was through his introduction that I met GMB, the writer who still means more to me than any other). The salt of the earth does not come any purer, any saltier, than George Garson, and I was never anything other than enriched by every moment of his company. He came into my life like an onshore gale while I was still a newspaper journalist, a gale which blasted many of my more timid ideas about writing, art – and life – into smithereens, and which urged me relentlessly along the path I have followed since.

⊙ ⊙ ⊙

It is the 29th of November, 2016. The low-slung, low-curving whalebacks of this south-west corner of the Pentlands are sunlit, snow-lit and frosted, and in the deepest recesses of the Medwin Water's banks, low-bowing blades of grass have been transformed by ice, the green sliver at the heart of each gleaming icicle as gloriously incarcerated as a pearl in an oyster. I have never seen these hills wear a fairer face than this. I am here because on this of all days I have business up the Medwin Water, but inevitably he is here too, in every whispering waterfall, in every fold of the ground, in every footfall. We have been here before, you see. The first time was when he told me the story and then showed me the landscape of the Covenanter's Grave. And this of all days is 350 years to the day since the Covenanter in question was laid in that grave.

Ah, sweet Medwin Water! A mouthful soothes the back of my throat. Another handful splashed in my face is a kind of renewal, a symbolic gesture of homage to what will always be George Garson's landscape in my mind. I simply borrow it occasionally, as I have done since the passage of time caught up with him, and he charged me with the responsibility of keeping an eye on the place and reporting back to him. Now, I mutter a word or two of thanks for all that was shared here, all that is gratefully remembered.

Walkers are fewer in this corner of the hills than in the over-promoted, mob-handed acres of the Pentland Hills Regional Park in the north. George was its sworn enemy, a regular and fluent curser of what "they" did to the hills he grew up with, for he was an Edinburgh south-sider by birth. The few folk you meet down here tend to be solitary chiels like himself, not given to walking the hills in parties, fond of the hills' solaces and silences, yet cheerful enough when you do pass the time of day with them because they know the chances are you are of the same cast.

We (I am something of a lone wolf in this regard too) like

to think we take our cues from the hills themselves. They meet our needs. We mould our moods to theirs: if they are hunkered down through a week of anti-cyclonic gloom, we go deep and dark ourselves. And if they celebrate winter's early arrival with sun and frosted snow, see how we glitter in response! They are subtler hills than their northern kin, wide-open on the surface, and given to concealing the best of themselves among the smaller intimacies of cleuch and syke. It was a thick, Lowland Scots tongue that named this landscape – Black Birn, Yield Brae, Lingy Knowe, Bawdy Moss, Bassy Burn, Fingerstane Cleuch. The hills around the north-south course of Medwin Water – Bleak Law, Black Law, Darlees Rig, Catstone Hill, Fadden Hill, Millstone Rig – rise easily in wide, airy curves until they are ultimately gathered in by the twin heights of Craigengar and Byrehope Mount. For all that these twins barely graze the 1,700-foot contour, they wear their overlordship of this land bravely enough, and in a glazed ermine of two-day-old snow they would pass for anyone's idea of mountain royalty. They despatch their various waters far and wide across the face of south Scotland: Medwin Water is a tributary of the River Clyde, Lyne Water to the east of it is bound for the Tweed, and to the north of that high ground, the first flickering burns of the Water of Leith set sail for the very heart of distant Edinburgh, thence to the River Forth at Leith.

There is a roof-of-the-world-ish feel to these wide-open heights. George Garson would tell you they are painted with broad brushstrokes and restricted palette. Then, warmed by my question, he would tell me what he meant, gesturing with an artist's hands at shadows that implied but did not reveal the hidden gully, and clasping an imaginary brush he reeled off the five different shades of grey on offer from almost blue to almost purple to almost black; then with his hand in front of his face he would rub a thumb repeatedly across the tips of two fingers to denote the landscape's texture, sinew, pith. He not only preferred these hills to the more sharply etched summits of the regional park like East and West Kip and Scald Law, he also preferred them to Highland mountains of the far north-west and the Cairngorms, where I had been his guide. At its root, the attraction of the Pentland Hills was one of kinship, of belonging. He slipped in among these hills with the ease of a hand in a cashmere glove; only Orkney endowed him with something comparable. I am as sure as I can be in his absence that he embraced with his artist's eye, as well as the twin strands of belonging, the comparable shapes of these low, whaleback hills and Orkney's low, whaleback islands. In his heart and his mind and his eye and his mind's eye, nowhere on Earth moved him like these Pentland Hills of home except for those Pentland Firth islands of home to untold generations of Garsons.

His favourite ploy in his hillwalking prime was a fifteen-mile-long circuit of his own devising, beginning and ending at Dunsyre, and stitching together all his preferences and prejudices into that singular journey among that herd of hills that gathers above and around sweet Medwin Water. He – and I (for he shared it with me occasionally) – loved it best in winter when the landscape wore an acutely primitive air and a smoky blue cast (but can you see the yellow within that smoky blue, I hear him speir at me, and in time I learned to see it), and when it necessarily consumed all the meagre daylight hours at our disposal. We emerged at the end of it all physically tried (but not found wanting) and spiritually supercharged by the terrain, the wide-open hilltop winds, and the old snow's tendency to linger longest and deepest between the hills where it smoothed over the ditches, burns, sykes and boggy holes, and it became something of a dishonour to escape without sinking at least one boot up to the knee, and preferably two. And that first time, then, he showed me the Covenanter's Grave, and told the immortal story of who lies buried there.

With the benefit of 350 years of hindsight, and especially on such a breathless late November morning as this (when nature will always provide the only religion I will ever need), the Covenanters' place in the history of Scotland strikes me as much ado about very little, and poor reason to shed blood, to kill and to die. It had all begun in 1637. King Charles I, a Stuart king of all things, had introduced the Book of Common Prayer, an episcopalian invention of all things, and decreed that it would be used throughout Britain. Opposition would be interpreted as treason. The Presbyterian Church of Scotland, for which episcopalianism was not too far removed from the work of the Devil, duly declared its opposition. In 1638 it drew up the National Covenant, to be signed by everyone who was opposed to the interference of the kings of Britain in the affairs of the Presbyterian Church of Scotland. Scots signed up in their thousands and thousands.

Sympathetic ministers, caught between a rock and a very hard place indeed, were evicted from their churches, and so they sought secret places where they could continue to preach, and so began the relationship between the Covenanters and the quiet places of the hills. But it didn't stop there. Those who failed to attend local church services were branded "rebels", and rebels were rounded up by Government troops. Many were fined or tortured, or both, and confronted with a simple choice: swear an oath acknowledging the king as head of the Church, or face execution. By the time Charles II took charge of things the land was pockmarked with countless skirmishes and battles. Among the hostilities, the so-called Pentlands Rising of 1666 consisted of a series of skirmishes that culminated in the hopelessly one-sided Battle of Rullion Green on November 28th of that year – 350 years and one day before I found myself slaking my thirst in the Medwin Water. The Covenanter army, if it can be called that, had mustered in the south-west of Scotland and travelled by way of Lanark to the Pentlands en route to Edinburgh. What they hoped to achieve there, only their God knows. There were 900 of them, and at Rullion Green on the eastern edge of the Pentlands near Penicuik, they were intercepted by a Government army of 3,000 men. One hundred Covenanters were killed in the battle, 300 more as they fled the battlefield, 120 were taken prisoner to Edinburgh where many were executed, while a handful were sent to be hanged in the south-west as an example to the natives.

So far, so very history textbook. But then there was John Carphin, and his story is the reason why I have come back, for he it is who lies in the Covenanter's Grave, up by on the summit crest of Black Law.

Carphin was an Ayrshire man, and he had marched with the Covenanters to Rullion Green. He was badly wounded, but somehow he eluded the mopping-up operation that killed the 300 fleeing men. From Rullion Green to Black Law is about twelve miles in a straight line, but any reasonable route between the two is going to be nearer fifteen miles, and as I have already explained, I have some experience of walking fifteen miles among these southern Pentland Hills in winter, and I hadn't just marched from the south-west of Scotland, fought a battle, then suffered a wound so serious that I would be dead within twenty-four hours; and nor were the hills awash with Government troops in a fever of bloodlust.

None of that deterred him. He had one idea in his head. It was that he should stay alive long enough and travel far enough towards the south-west so that he could reach, or at least see, the hills of Ayrshire; just possibly, he might make it all the way back to his own hills of home and die there in peace. Given where he ended up in the dead of night at Medwinhead on the Medwin Water, it would seem that he knew enough of the Pentlands topography to find his way back to the Lanark Road, but he was still four miles short of it when he stumbled into the arms of a Samaritan.

Adam Sanderson was a shepherd who lived at Blackhill, an isolated cottage on the banks of the Medwin. Carphin was far gone when Sanderson found him, and the shepherd made to take him in and tend his wounds as best he could. But Carphin declined. He reasoned that Sanderson's life would be endangered for harbouring a fugitive Covenanter – an amazing show of concern for his fellow man considering what he himself had just been through. One must assume that he knew by then that he was breathing his last, that the Ayrshire hills were out of reach to him, and it seems that he then asked Sanderson to bury him in sight of his homeland.

The two men sheltered for a while under an oak, and it was there that Carphin died. Sanderson carried him up to the summit slopes of Black Law, a distance of perhaps half a mile and an ascent of 300 feet. From there, there is a sightline through a gap in the hills between Bleak Law and The Pike, and at its furthest reach, eighteen miles distant, is a glimpse of Ayrshire hills. He marked the spot with a rough stone, on which was carved a coded message, one the Covenanters would understand, but which would baffle the dragoons if any of them chanced that way. That stone is now in Dunsyre Kirk, and at the Covenanter's Grave there is a tombstone erected around 1840. By then, there had already been a bizarre sequel, which was reported in *Blackwood's Magazine* of October 1817:

> *An enterprising youth, a farmer's son in the Easdon district* [Easton, a farm near Dunsyre], *went to the top of the hill with a spade with a view to discovering whether tradition was correct in declaring that this spot was the Covenanter's Grave. He began to dig, and speedily found what he was after. He came home in triumph with a skull, some pieces of cloth, and a few brass buttons, but his father, a true-blue Presbyterian, indignant at the desecration of a spot hallowed to the mind of every patriotic Scotsman, first administered a severe thrashing to his son, and then went with him to re-inter the sacred relics ...*

A minister of Dunsyre, a Dr Manuel, eventually acted on a proposal to create a permanent monument, and at his own expense the tombstone was erected where it still stands. And around 1990, George Garson copied out the inscription and set it at the start of his own poem to Adam Sanderson: "sacred to the memory of a covenanter who fought and was wounded at Rullion Green Nov 28th, 1666, and who died at Oaken Bush the day after the Battle and was buried here by Adam Sanderson of Blackhill."

BEFORE THE BATTLE

Come first light, his commonplace skyline
ran mad with curses and pikes.

He had slept fitfully on his strae bed,
listening …

The nocturnal raspings of stoat and rat
riven by the alien tongues and the yelp of steel.

A gaunt straggle:
some had guns with rusty ratches;
others the coulter of a plough,
scythes and spades.
Some had halbards, forks and flails.

'The Almichty bless the shiel, hird.
Nae ill tae ye guidman.
Oor fecht lies furth o' your bit dykes and fanks.
But pray for us.
For Presbyterian bluid micht weel smitch
your puckle knows gin dayset.'

Weaned on the moor's elemental creed,
he mumbled rough blessing on the day

and called his dog to heel,
flummoxed by the grim tenets of Kirk and Covenant.

Inching into sleep that night,
he pondered on the Westland man:
a shilpit chiel,
yellow hair slaggered to his brow
by winter's ceaseless blash,
legs clad in hoggers of strae
bound with rags.
Unaware that, come dawn,
he'd spade down the bairn's sword-bitten corpse
in a shallow hillside grave.

I concede that I am still as "flummoxed by the grim tenets of
Kirk and Covenant" as Adam Sanderson was 350 years ago,
and "the moor's elemental creed" is a surer star to steer by for
me too, as it was for him. Yet it is impossible to be unmoved
by his selfless response to the plight of John Carphin, as
impossible as it is to be unmoved by Carphin's concern for
his would-be rescuer; an exchange of mutual old-world
courtesy between two such different men of the hills. And I
am well aware that I used the word "Samaritan" back there
to introduce Sanderson, and there are few more potent
symbols of the Christian faith than the Good Samaritan. But
to go to war over a book of prayer, to die and to kill because
you believe your take on that faith is better – truer – than
someone else's … "flummoxed" is the right word. Why not,
for example, pay lip service to episcopalianism in the kirk
building, and keep the old ways alive in those secret meetings

in the hills until the fuss died down, until they could be reintroduced by stealth, until some other king from some other dynasty or other came up with another daft idea of the true faith, or an enlightened one who simply repealed the stain of the daftness?

But it is hard to deny the beauty and the tranquil atmosphere of the little kirk at Dunsyre, and I have never passed that way without pausing to push open the door and touch the old stone, the original one with its coded carving, and to acknowledge what passed up the valley of the Medwin Water that day and night in 1666. This was my starting point again, that earliest winter morning of 2016, in the shadow of Dunsyre Hill, which my old friend so revered. His God alone knows how many times he climbed it, drew it and otherwise committed it to the inner sanctum of memory. Ten years before, I had visited him and Jean at their home in the West Lothian village of East Burnside, and a decent stone's throw from the Lanark Road and the west flank of the Pentlands. He handed me a big charcoal drawing. Its title, written on the back, is *The Path to the Mountain*. It is a rough drawing, done quickly, and his instruction to me was that if I wanted to put it on a wall I should just stick it up with Blu-Tack, because it wasn't worth framing, and for a few years I did just that. He said it was a hill of his imagination but that Dunsyre Hill was in the back of his mind. But after he died, and a retrospective exhibition of his work was being organised, involving the framing of a considerable body of late work, I added it to the framer's workload, and now it hangs in a more dignified setting in my house, and I take it as a kind of constant injunction from the artist that I should keep following the path to the mountain, whether it's lowly Dunsyre Hill or Bràigh Riabhach or Suilven, or my friendly neighbourhood mountain of Ben Ledi, or, as on the morning of November 29th, 2016, Black Law. So I raised a hand to Dunsyre Hill and set off for sweet Medwin Water one more time. And when I reached its banks and turned north to fall in with its amiable company and downed a ceremonial dram of its water from my cupped hand, I guessed that the nature of winter would never taste sweeter than this, no matter where its journey took me.

Improbably, Adam Sanderson's Blackhill cottage still stands, or at least the footprint of it does. What survives is a low ruin, less than waist-high in places. I stopped there to look at the stonework and to see if I could still detect the places where a kind of rough restoration had been applied in patches. This was George's homage to Sanderson, long before he wrote the poem. His years of studying the architecture and the archaeology of Orkney, and applying what he learned there to his slate mosaics, not to mention his great enthusiasm for the Pentlands' repertoire of wonderfully worked drystane dykes …all that had given him a certain easy familiarity with, and a fluency for the craft of setting stone on stone so that it "reads". He may have wrought his art and his poetry from Orkney bedrock, but he understood the timeless strength that underpins it too. And besides, he'd built ships.

The passing of time, the blessing of lichen, and the cold fire of many a winter wind, had absorbed his handiwork into the body of the ruin and I couldn't tell his stonework from the rest of what remains of Blackhill, and I dare say he would judge that I could pay him no higher compliment.

The Medwin is a heron's water, and in the same way, the heron is a Pentlands bird. The myriad burns, cleuchs, sykes, bogs and reservoirs fill these hills with small fish, frogs, toads and other heron food. I had been sitting for a while by Sanderson's ruin, and when I finally stood and advanced a few yards towards the water, a heron I had not seen and which had not seen me, rose from the burn with a ponderous heave of a wingspan that looks more than is strictly necessary to do the job. As it rose from shadow into sunlight, its unfolded legs scattered pinpricks of watery light, its shadow rippled across the decrepit stone walls of Blackhill, and suddenly my memory was turning cartwheels. I had seen that simple shadow-dance before.

George Garson and I were padding up the Medwin, rounding the scrap of a pinewood that clings there, dropping down through the worn-out bracken to the burn, when a heron rose from a pool, spread a grey-blue sailcloth of wings, and as he climbed, I saw his shadow fall across the walls of Sanderson's cottage. It was done within a few seconds, but it had caught my eye as it clambered the slope up to the ruin, and I had turned to George and shouted:

"The shadow!"

For the sight of it had stopped me dead, and the thought it implanted was this:

How many shadows of how many herons have fallen across these walls throughout the life and long death of the cottage of Blackhill? Say 400 years? When there was a roof on the walls, Sanderson would see the shadow slide down it whenever a heron dropped down to the pool. He would see an otter's wake bubbling upstream, and he would see the shadow climb the house again as the heron leapt in slow alarm with a Presbyterian oath of its own. I have no doubt that from time to time the shadow would wear the embellishment of an eel at the sharp end (the immortal Henry Williamson referred to it as "a two-pointed spear on a shaft hidden by long, narrow feathers"), as the bird was disturbed while it wrestled with its catch. There are few things in nature less willing to die than an eel in a Scottish hill burn. In that way, or some other, thousands of heron shadows have darkened Sanderson's window and scaled his walls and the pitch of his roof.

The particular heron George and I disturbed that day had, in its turn, disturbed a dipper from a mid-stream rock. There are few more eloquently displayed extremes of the diverse art of bird flight than these – the ponderous heave of heron wings and the tiny headlong blur of the burn-clinging dipper. Yet when the dipper goes underwater-hunting, his wings slow to a heron's gait as he dives down, effortlessly defying all the instincts of natural buoyancy, and he drags his shadow down with him to walk along the river bed. On the bank, we grounded bipeds watched with a kind of stupefied wonder.

I hefted a few stones as if I knew what I was doing and set them thoughtfully into the wall of Blackhill, but I don't know what I'm doing and they never seem to find a snug fit. It's the thought that counts now, as far as that particular ruin is concerned. It has ceased to be Sanderson's place, and instead it has become a landmark in George Garson's territory, in George Garson's Pentlands, which is how he thought of it himself. I headed off uphill into the sun and the cold, still air and the brilliance of snow-light. I paused at Carphin's final resting place, his plain stone graced by a thin arch of frozen snow, and here and there patches of the same snow still clung to the inscribed face of the stone like white lichen, eccentrically editing its text: *...and who di … …sh/ the day a … …e Battle/ and w … …uried here …*

I hope he found his peace and his God, and I hope his God was generous to him. Whatever the nature of the reason why you died, John Carphin, there are worse places by far to be laid to rest, even if it isn't Ayrshire.

So I had paid my small tribute to the events of the day after the Battle of Rullion Green and to the landscape which had witnessed them, and I had honoured the memory of the man who introduced me to Carphin's story and to the douce hills that feed sweet Medwin Water. And then the day's focal point was behind me. I turned away from his stone and looked around. A wide plateau tilts gently north-wards from Black Law to White Craig, and I had the place to myself. For want of anything more pressing or fulfilling to do, I walked north, content in my solitude. An elemental simplicity fell into place as I walked, for I simply walked for the pleasure of walking, of just being in that landscape for that moment. There was a line of old footprints in the snow and I followed these in the general direction of White Craig. From time to time, circumstances conspire in this nature-writing life to create a space, an emptiness of a kind, but a fertile emptiness in which a self-sown seed begins to stir into life and an idea begins to grow. And somewhere between Black Law and White Craig, the day gently slipped its moorings and sailed away without me. In its departing wake I stepped beyond landscape, beyond time, into a sphere of complete freedom. At first, it was perhaps the product of a kind of aimlessness, but I rarely keep nature's company without a purpose of my own or one that nature imposes on me. It only ever happens in winter, in an undemanding landscape where the eye suddenly finds nowhere to linger, where the sky is more of a presence than the land, and that sky devoid of all cloud and almost all colour; so it is rare, and then travel becomes a thing of the mind. What arose was the idea that I was following footsteps that were many years old, in the snows of all time. Norman MacCaig voiced the idea in a poem following the death of his great friend A.K. MacLeod in Assynt: *He is gone: but you can see / his tracks still, in the snow of the world.* So perhaps something of the nature of the day imbued a line of footprints in the snow with a particular significance, a spectre composed of all those who walked here between, say, Garson and Sanderson, Carphin for that matter, all of them urged on by motives of their own. But the direction they ushered me along was not what you might have expected.

A few years ago now, I was looking for a new way into a story I was trying to write. What I finally settled on emerged from circumstances not unlike these in which I now found myself. I had been walking a high, broad and featureless ridge on a day which had long since lost its purpose: I had been looking for golden eagles and instead I encountered only a single south-making whooper swan. Later, eagle-less and (almost) swan-less, I was taken aback by the apparent knowledge that I was walking in old south-making foot-steps. They were not the footsteps of the day before or the weekend before, but rather of many years before. I inhabited the footprints as if I were the print-maker. In my mind, then, he became a shape-shifter from the far north of the world, a poet and storyteller from a mountain country where swan legends were born and endure – swans becoming people, people becoming swans. He was on a kind of pilgrimage, following a command from a tribal elder to spend a winter furth of mountains, so that he might see them "through the eyes of those who live beyond".

That story became a short novel, *The Mountain of Light* (Whittles, 2003), and it was set between the Stirling Castle rock and Ben Ledi, the handsome pyramidal mountain which dominates the north-west skyline from Stirling. By that time, these two conspicuous landmarks where Highland and Lowland Scotland collide had become central to my everyday life. And suddenly, walking that modest Pentland Hills plateau fifteen years later, first Norman MacCaig's lines crept into my mind, followed at once by the vivid recollection of the day I stepped in the spoor of the old swan-wanderer. We had not met since the day I finished writing the book.

I never reached White Craig. Instead, and without any conscious decision, I drifted west of north from the heart of the plateau to its highest point at Darlees Rig. Then the very last steps to the summit burst the world apart, and there, far in the north-west, were the Highland mountains arrayed in a gently curving arc, a frieze of miniaturised mountain shapes, all acutely sculpted angles, snow brilliance and deep blue shadows; and with Ben Ledi for its centre-piece. I snapped back into the here and now of the situation. It felt like a summons.

I consulted my fifty-year-old map, confirmed a compass bearing, raised a farewell hand to the men whose finished lives had lured me here. Then I dropped down from that airy place to the West Water and kept its murmuring company until it met the path back to Dunsyre. All the way home, I tried to reconvene something of that day with the single swan and the old, old footsteps, and what flowed from it, but found it tantalisingly elusive. Late in the evening, with my preferred winter whisky in my hand, I sat down with that old book and renewed acquaintance with the nameless wanderer of *The Mountain of Light*.

Chapter Four

The Well-Being of Mountain People is my Purpose

(from *The Mountain of Light*)

MANY MEN WERE RESTLESS in those difficult days between the wars. Many a tramp and wanderer forsook downcast town and city lives and took to the lonely roads of the Scottish Highlands. Nature's quietude among the mountains was the certainty they craved through that least certain of times.

It was a hospitable land then, unsuspicious of travellers and their motives, ignorant of tourism. Simple truths held sway. A solitary wanderer could travel, eat, sleep, albeit primitively, for next to nothing. Next to nothing was what most of them had, but they judged that richer than the nothing they had left behind. Such a wanderer might pay his dues with a story, a song, gossip gleaned on the road. These might buy him a bite, a bed, a pair of old boots with an untrodden mile or two left in them.

Often, that mysterious grapevine that whispers among Highland places would travel before him, announcing his arrival at the next village or township or farm. But there was one wanderer who captivated the grapevine as much as he taxed its powers.

He was tall and larch-straight. White hair fell to his broad shoulders or bannered out behind him when he faced the wind – "like a white wing," said an old one who nodded courteously to him on a north coast cliff path. His body was agile and lean, length of his stride as full as a stag's. But his face looked older than his body, for it had weathered under the stings of many winds. His long sealskin coat was grey and looked like a robe. His speech bounced strangely on wide vowels and hard gutturals, a voice that sprang on the craning ear of the grapevine with the rhythms and music you might have heard in the Shetland of a century before, an antiquated lilt. A few coastal villagers, old hauled-out mariners who once went whaling in northern oceans, swore it was Iceland they heard in his voice; others said no, it was Faroe, or Norway, or Spitsbergen. They agreed at least about the hemisphere, and that his eyes were the eerie ice-green of glaciers.

Then, there were his stories.

Such stories! And with these he would spellbind uneasy hosts wherever he paused. Stories of northern places imprisoned by mountains in a way no Highland places are. They told of poets in mountain places. Often they told of swans (fearful glances among a few old Highlanders at that, for it was the troubled lot of the aged and wise to see through the swan stories), swans that wove their flights through the lives of mortals and interwove with their very existences, mortal becoming swan, swan becoming mortal.

In one village after another, people shook their head at these stories, but the grapevine was enthralled despite itself, and the wanderer was asked for them again and again wherever he paused on his journey south, always south.

The swan stories troubled them for reasons they were slow to acknowledge. Indeed, they may not have been able to articulate them at all, for the reasons were rooted deep and distant, inherited from earlier eras than theirs, eras when a swan was held to be the guardian of a human's mortal soul, that when man, woman or child died, their souls flew on immortally, within swans.

It was also held that swan could become mortal, that changelings – poor enslaved creatures – walked the land between flightings. So you never turned away nor gave offence to the swan-folk. You could never be sure, and there was no way of knowing.

To add to the unease some felt, the wanderer seemed to arrive in the landscape unpredictably, eluding the instincts of the grapevine, confounding its best guesses, troubling that fine line that skirts the frayed edge of folklore and unchancy eye-witness. So half-submerged instincts stirred strangely.

Sometimes the wanderer would use the old ways through the hills that people had trodden for as long as there had been people. But at other times he would pass through a landscape unseen and then some would say he had travelled by night and some would say he flew, and both were hallmarks of the swan-folk.

From Strathy Point on Scotland's northmost mainland shore to Strathyre in Perthshire near the southmost beginning and end of the mountains, his travels held to their relentless southerly course. That too was curious, for it suggested he had the purpose of destination, whereas the wandering was destination enough for most of the Highlands' wayfarers.

They still say in Strathyre that it was an old hill shepherd, who had travelled the world's mountains himself and fetched up on that Highland Edge to while away his last years … that it was he who determined the ultimate course of events which befell the wanderer. But all up and down the route of his travels through Scotland, the old ones who saw him said his destination was predetermined and beyond his control. That he was driven. And that too was the way things were for the swan-folk, or so the old handed-down stories told it.

There is some persuasive evidence that the shepherd passed the time of day with him on a hill shoulder west of the village a bit. The wanderer, it seems, had taken to the high ground again, stag-striding out along that south-bound shoulder, shunning the easier going along Loch Lubnaigside. If you had heard the story of that portentous meeting told by the Strathyre folk for a generation or two after the event, you would gather that the shepherd had a good ear for the grapevine, and might have greeted the wanderer thus:

"So, still south, is it?"

"Still south," the wanderer smiled.

"Well, if you're holding south all day, and you're as thirled to the mountains as I think you are, there is only one left after this wee hill shoulder."

He pointed to where a singular cone stood slightly aloof from all that landscape, the first and last mountain of the Highlands.

"What is its name, this signposting mountain?" the wanderer asked.

"Ben Ledi."

"Ledi? A strange name for a southern mountain. What does it mean?"

"It's obscure now. Some swear it means the Mountain of God, others the Mountain of Light."

"And what do you say? You must know it as well as anyone. God or Light?"

"I say it's much the same thing. All we can ask of our Gods is that they shed a little light on the road ahead."

The wanderer smiled again, and added, "Indeed. Or the road behind?"

"That can be useful too. Frankly, a good light is more use to me than any God I ever heard of."

The wanderer, you may be sure, had a thoughtful ear for the conversation of the local people he met along the way, hearing them as eagerly as they heard his stories. He saw in them, it would seem, some kind of last hope for the mountain realm, a hope of guardianship. He had told the Strathyre folk (and doubtless many others on his way south):

"The well-being of mountain people is my purpose on the road. That and the well-being of the mountain."

That afterthought had baffled as many as it intrigued. The shepherd, though, had heard it the night before in the village inn, heard the note of kinship it struck in him, and he saw now the quickening of this wanderer's interest. He said:

"Mine is a seeing job. A good light breaks up the contours into watchable fragments. The hidden ledges are revealed where a beast might stand or fall, or an eagle might nest or a fox lie up. Mostly there is good light in these mountains. A God, forever peering down through the clouds, is in no position to assist, for all that I ask one often enough."

"And what do *you* do," asked the wanderer, "if your seeing reveals a nesting eagle or a lying-up fox?"

"I watch, of course. I watch how *they* see. They – the eagle and the fox in that order – are the best at the seeing job in the mountains. It may be, of course, that they do not see as far *back* as swans."

"Shepherd," said the wanderer, "it has been good to talk to you. You are an extraordinary shepherd for a land such as this. What is your name?"

The shepherd nodded formally:

"John Muir, at your service."

"I have heard of a John Muir who was a shepherd and poet of the mountains, although I hardly expected to meet him here."

"As I hardly expected to find a swan-pilgrim. The swan things have been submerged even longer than the wolf. People are unsure, now that you have let the light of swan-flight into their eyes. The old ones know the stories. The young ones scoff. They will take some convincing. But I think I see what is at work within you. Wherever your journey leads, I hope there is a Light or a God – whatever pleases you – to illuminate the next good mile and the next. And a strong white wing when you need uplifting."

The glacier-green eyes of the wanderer turned to the one mountain shape which still lay to the south.

"The Mountain of Light. There can surely be no better place to let it end."

The mountain commands all that land. It stands above the throat of a pass, the first and last thoroughfare of the High-lands. It marks a watershed of landscapes. Near its summit lies a small watersheet, Lochan Nan Corp, which is the Lochan of the Corpse. A child's body was found there amid a smothering of swan feathers. It was said that he had been claimed by the swan-folk, and that in many guises (but mostly as a single whooper swan – the Icelandic race that winters in Scotland) he still returned to the lochan during the quiet hours of dusk and dawn when he might linger secure from human gaze, and mourning that which was lost.

The wanderer came late in the afternoon to the lochan, a solitary figure on the back of the mountain. He stood there for an hour and only his coat and his hair moved in the wind. He looked as rooted as a tree. His silence matched his stillness. Then he climbed to the last mountain summit and there he thanked his own light-shedding God, for he believed at that moment he had been delivered from a great torment.

He had only ever known mountain lands, locked in the places of the northlands of the Earth where the ice was still as much of an element as rock and wind and water and fire. Now he saw a broad river valley, its harvested fields a chequer of pale gold in lowering sunlight. A long wall of low, flat-topped hills held the valley to the south, and where the valley opened to the east he saw where fields and river yielded to the supremacy of single mighty rock. There the sun stoked pale fires in the surmounting walls of a great castle.

That rock drew him. His was an eye long accustomed to reading landscapes, so that he could penetrate the inscapes which are the unseen skeletal structures and foundations within and beneath all landscapes. Just as a good architect might gaze on a great building and marvel at the unseen genius of its construction as well as the beauty of the façade, so he could comprehend the hand of nature as architect in the midst of its great works.

So he appraised the far-off rock and its flat-bottomed river valley thus:

"First the volcano spat and roared and cloaked itself in heaps of its own spoil, then it cooled. Then it shed its useless loosening outer layers and reinvented itself, cold and alone, the naked rock.

"Next the ice, the great ice that carved the valley but baulked at the cold rock, gripped it but could not overwhelm it.

"Next the sea. These two, ice and sea, shaped the waist of this land. The ice melted, the sea flowed and flowed until it acknowledged an unyielding mountain chain, these mountains where I stand, a protecting arm about the waist.

"The sea relented. As it withdrew eastwards again, it also deferred to that one cold rock. The rock remains, the volcano's souvenir, hewn and coughed up out of the valley's oldest darkness. The ice was too new and no match for it. But neither was the sea, and that is more remarkable, for it is rare in an island landscape for a rock to wear down the sea.

"So the sea parted, swam round the rock, fell back and back. Now, instead of the ice, instead of the sea, a great river flows, a water snake, deep and dark and coiled. Its strength is fed by the benevolence of these mountains, and they are its kin, for they too were once the ice's tortured prisoners, worn and wearied down to the nub.

"Men came.

"Where the sea had fallen back and back they found the valley, fertile and sheltered by mountainside and hillside. They would marvel at the one cold rock, at its command of the country in all directions, at its prospects to the mountains, at the great river below it (their safe passage to and from the sea whence they had come). Was there a sounder place in all the land to fortify and settle? There was none. So they claimed the rock for their own, built a wooden fortress there, then a succession of bigger and better wooden fortresses, then a great stone castle that still stands, then a walled town that spilled downhill from the plinth to a bridge over the river, a causeway beyond the bridge across the sodden valley to the foothills, the mountains beyond."

So that was the rock the wanderer set eyes on from the summit of the Mountain of Light, twenty miles distant. The rock had long since been named – Stirling. But once it was called Strivelin, which some say is the Place of Strifes, after all the warrings of nature the rock had endured. It would prove a prophetic name as well as a historic one, for in the agonising birth throes, life throes and death throes of Scotland as an independent nation, the rock watched a parade ground of battlefields assemble and disassemble in its shadow, licking its myriad wounds. If you held the rock and its castle, you held the key to the kingdom, or so men thought once, but the key to their Scotland was never so simple as that, and it has long since rusted in the unfathomable lock of the Union, all but immovable it seemed, more elusive than ever, although who knew what winds of change might blow in from the sea, down from the mountains?

The wanderer saw and sensed a change in the land. It was as the shepherd Muir had told him. There was no mountain beyond this one, and he sensed that the values and priorities common to all mountain lands would also be absent in the valley. In their place, what?

Perhaps it was then he saw a white ripple go through the far fields and knew it for a skein of whooper swans, for the Icelandic whoopers fall from the mountain skies and linger in the valley winter-long. The birds' presence surely reassured him, so that when he went down at last, down to the valley the people called the Carse, he would go eagerly. And from that Carse the Place of Strifes beckoned peacefully enough. There, he reasoned, the Highland grapevine would have lost its thread, for the place stood alone in its own realm, neither Highland nor Lowland, and walled in only by the low hills to the south, the mountains to the north and west. Whatever else, it would be a place with its own story.

An old crone's words were in his ears as he climbed down and felt the floor of the Carse flatten under his feet, words from a distant time, a distant mountain land:

"Absorb all that the mountains can give you, but then stand for a winter beyond the furthest edge of the mountains. Cross that bridge of landscapes. See the mountains with the eyes of those who live beyond."

⊙ ⊙ ⊙

Re-reading that chapter from *The Mountain of Light* now, re-introducing myself to this strange wanderer-poet of a character I invented about fifteen years ago, I don't have very far to look for his origins. The northlands of the Earth, the tribe of wild swans, and the poetry of the land are three of the most enduring elements of my fascination for nature.

Although I was born and brought up in Dundee (and I have never stopped thinking of it as home), I have evolved over the years into an uneasy townsman. Throughout my nature-writing years, I have worked from a base either in Stirling itself or in the mountain realms of Glen Dochart and Balquhidder in Stirling's north-west hinterland. I have adopted and grown into that Highland Edge territory with Ben Ledi at its heart and embracing the Carse of Stirling to its south and the mountains immediately to its north, east and west, all their lochs and rivers and forests. A kind of intimacy springs from the constant reworking of known circumstances, and because I have done it for so long now (almost thirty years), I have a sense of the rhythms to which nature moves across the landscape. It is unsurprising then, that, I should reach for that landscape for my first novel of the land, and centre it on the travels of a wandering, solace-seeking swan-poet who thinks he might find what he is looking for in a rock-founded settlement just beyond the mountains.

The view across the Carse to that arc of mountains is Stirling's great gift to a nature writer. One December morning, I was walking below the castle by the 17th-century King's Knot, strangely sculpted earthworks which delineate the form of a garden created in 1627–9 for Charles I within what was then a royal hunting park. The castle on its sheer rock towers above the King's Knot, and from that ancient garden's raised and terraced centrepiece – and on the right kind of day – the frontier mountains of the Highlands appear at their most alluring. But at first glance, that December morning was the wrong kind of day. A kink of the jetstream that generated midnight gales and thudding rain squalls at

3a.m. had subsided into hefty winds and a frayed and torn-open sky. The mountains were shut in by massed clouds. Yet even on such days when the mountains are lost to the citizens' gaze, their absence reaches across the intervening miles with a measure of sustenance. Far in the west (where Ben Lomond's wide sprawl of mountain shoulders had been smothered in a smouldering bruise-shaded shroud), strange shafts of rain-and-snow clouds appeared to fan outwards and upwards across the sky from a kind of low, crab-shaped hub, like the aurora borealis in reverse. That hub was suddenly galvanised by a burst of low sunlight from over my left shoulder, and a ragged patch of rainbow jived there for all of two minutes, a hypnotic dance.

The big wind was driving the light show both in the south and the west. In the south, it force-fed low, winter-white sunlight into holes among fast clouds, so that the light was never still. In the west, dense showers marched round the arc of the mountains as they so often do. As flashing sunlight worked on them, a mobile, patchy rainbow travelled among them. When it reached Ben Ledi, the nearest of the mountains, there was a sudden tear in the shroud, a sudden glimpse into the tormented mountain world beyond, a sudden revelation of the summit pyramid draped in snow. Seconds later the rainbow passed across it and seemed to have the effect of healing the breach, for as it danced on, the mountain vanished again, the clouds lowered, thickened and darkened, and advanced on the foothills.

Through it all, the wide, flat sprawl of the Carse, its grass-land farms, its slow, coiled river, its small woods and its patches of standing floodwater ... all that lay in a kind of stupefied calm. Patches of sunlight flared and dowsed everywhere, but nothing else moved. It was as if nature had its hands full of sky and mountain and storm, and the needs of these were all-consuming.

Stirling was designed by nature to be a fulcrum in Scotland's story, the belt-buckle at her waist clasping Highlands and Lowlands together, a fortified glacial plug guarding the only usable crossing of the Forth if you were a king with an army, and whether defending or invading. As a result, the native-born sons and daughters are Sons of the Rock and Daughters of the Rock. So there are elements in the make-up of the place that appeal to the kind of writer I have become. The proximity and the permanence of mountains is the foremost of these, a relationship that colours much of my writing.

Chapter Five

A Diary of Early Winter

DECEMBER 2016 SETTLED INTO a yawn of mild gloom. That bejewelled foray in the Pentlands two days before might have been another country in another time zone. According to the Met Office, the 1st of December is also the first day of meteorological winter. It was clear at once that no one had told winter that year. Sometimes the solution to such pervasive and windless greyness lies in a short, sharp ascent from low to high ground. The shortest and sharpest available to me is via the south-facing slopes of the western edge of the Ochil Hills up onto the airy plateau of Sheriffmuir, whose historical claims to fame are a wretchedly indecisive battle of the 1715 Jacobite uprising in which Rob Roy MacGregor may or may not have participated, and an inn which was once home to a much more famous grizzly bear called Hercules. Today, the battlefield is more or less constantly under siege by the forestry industry, which seems to be obsessed with obliterating the undisciplined regime of heather-moor-and-scattered-Scots-pine, and replacing it with admirably disciplined ranks of non-Scots conifers drawn from the ranks of the usual forestry industry suspects. Sundry clan societies protest, but the clans hold fewer terrors for the establishment in the 21st century, and the forestry industry has more clout, more lawyers, and for that matter, more money.

Sheriffmuir's battlefield is an eerie place on such a day. The Gathering Stone lies prone and broken, and protected by an arched cage of metal bars from those mysterious elements of society who think it might be worth stealing. Its value, of course, is all symbolism, but it's hardly the Stone of Destiny, is it? I don't like battlefields, I never have, even when they have views of Highland mountains, as Sheriffmuir has on better days than this. The only one that ever moved me was Flodden, and I never rationalised why. Perhaps because James IV was killed there, and he was one of our better kings, although demonstrably he was a lousy soldier. Humanity's appetite for wars is its least appealing character trait, second only to its insistence on commemorating them so ostentatiously. I would dig up all the battlefields, remove their every memorial, demolish the wretched visitor centres of the more commercially-astute custodians (the National Trust for Scotland's coach-hungry money-spinners at Bannockburn and Culloden spring effortlessly to mind), and turn them all into nature reserves, but I have not attracted many followers to that particular crusade.

I left the sword-smitten ghosts of Sheriffmuir to their grim inheritance and went in search of some of the more life-affirming inhabitants of my doorstep hills. The second highest field of a particularly marginal species of farm just below the first slopes of the open hill ended in a wide swathe of rough ground. Tall, wild grass, withered wild flowers, and winter-bared scrub amounted to the kind of field edge where nature thrives. Beyond that was a fence and a shelter-belt of small, wind-tormented trees. Between the edge of the field and the fence was a long, narrow space the width of the whole field, a kind of roofless tunnel with the trees on one side and the tall grass on the other. I was driving slowly up the deserted single-track hill-road, window-down, half an eye on the road and one-and-a-half-eyes on the possibilities of the field.

A shape fell. That was all I saw. But it was enough to persuade me to pull over.

The first thing to establish was where it had fallen from. Then I spotted a wire – a telephone cable – slung on skinny poles across the top of the field. I guessed that was where the shape had been. I examined the terrain more carefully. I thought: if I had asked nature how to design a suitable terrain up here for a hunting sparrowhawk, it might have replied that ideally, it would like a kind of roofless tunnel between field and trees to facilitate a low-level, high-speed approach from which to launch an attack on, say, perched wood pigeons or thrushes or starlings or jackdaws on the wire, the fence or the trees; with the added option of a grasstop-level raid on large flocks of seed-feeders.

A small bird, a sparrow I think, blurred across my binocular lenses from right to left, or from field to trees, followed almost at once by a second blur, a slate-blue-and-orangey rasp of a blur. The first blur buried itself deep in the trees. The second baulked in front of the trees, rose in a phenomenally tight climbing turn and dropped to the ground inside the roofless tunnel. The bird was a dark shadow in a hall of shadows. Then it flew: a flat-out dash a foot off the ground fifty yards along the tunnel, then up *through* the grass to emerge into daylight a few inches above the grass, scattering small birds in every direction, and inciting a gruesomely discordant chorus of jackdaw and pheasant cries. There was a low and wide clockwise circle, which drew another blank, and it ended perched in full daylight on the fence and facing the field. Behold the male sparrowhawk in all his finery.

The back and the folded upper wings were more or less the same colour as the day's sky, a muted blue with strong overtones of grey. The closely barred breast was somewhere between reddish chestnut brown and burnt umber. In sunlight, which was quite absent at that moment, it can be deep orange, a breathtaking shade of flame in full flight.

But it is the sparrowhawk's eyes that you remember. Are there yellower eyes anywhere in the land than these? There are, after all, no wolves. Their black setting intensifies the shade, exaggerates their lethal potency. I suppose that from time to time, in this no man's land between hill and farm, sparrowhawk must lock eyes with short-eared owl, an exchange of intensity that surely generates a degree of mutual respect? On the other hand, the legs were long and skinny and a somehow less credible shade of yellow than the eyes, and just a little bit disappointing. They looked like they could be on a coot, for example, although I wouldn't say that out loud within the hawk's hearing. Its attitude changed from horizontal to vertical, suggesting it planned to hang around for a while, and once it had perched upright on the fence I could hardly see the legs, and the whole bird was an agreeable package of aesthetics.

Five minutes passed. Then ten. Then ten more. The hawk

made no attempt at concealment in that time, but I think that what he was doing was becoming a fragment of the landscape. I had noticed that over those few minutes, the small birds had come out of hiding and were once again seed-feeding in the field edge, the nearest of them not fifty yards from the motionless hawk. Patience and stillness is how you get close to nature, you let it come to you, and that is how you get results. It is as true for a nature writer as it is for a sparrowhawk. Then he flew, flat-out from a standing start, low over the grass, a quick flip of his left wing, down into the depths of the grass, from which he did not reappear, or if he did, I never saw him go.

High overhead, flying in the slowest of wide circles, a red kite had been watching proceedings for some time, watching from the wings you might say, for few birds appear to *inhabit* flight with such leisurely poise.

⊙ ⊙ ⊙

I had lunch with a raven. In this nature-writing life, it's the kind of thing that happens when you take your lunch for a walk. And taking lunch for a walk is always easy to justify to yourself even if it consumes three midday hours, because you end up sharing it with a raven and your lunch just served you up something quite unforeseen to write about, and that is the nature of the job after all. The first proper snow had come to the mountains two days since, and then it stopped and the temperature rose and the sun shone and I decided I would take lunch for a walk where I could see the mountains, before the snow vanished again.

I made for a low ridge, a topographical no man's land between Lowlands and Highlands. It is mostly plantation forest, but I know a way through that puts snowy, sunlit mountains at the far end of every gap in the trees. And given that the natives include pine martens, foxes, red squirrels, red deer, roe deer, buzzards, crossbills, siskins, jays and (the new kids on the block) nuthatches, there was always the chance that something would show up to prolong lunch. What showed up was the raven.

A wide-open area just below the ridge was recovering after felling operations. Not only have the fellers left stands of pine and larch and still-standing deadwood, they also revealed an unsuspected old footpath that tiptoes discreetly away from the main forest track. A mile along the path, I stopped on a still and sunny acre on top of the ridge, sat on a tree stump, and unpacked lunch. Then I heard the raven. The voice was a soft, hoarse contralto, well short of the characteristic, all-out, far-carrying "kruuk!", and I had trouble finding the source of the voice. But then it moved to a broken branch on a dead tree silhouetted against the sky and about a quarter of a mile away, and I found it as it fussily adjusted its stance. Then it called again.

Ravens are among the easier birds to mimic. They are also among the most eager call-and-response enthusiasts. So I called back while I watched through binoculars and saw its head turn in my direction. Soon we were chatting away in variations on a theme of "koo", "kroo", "kroo-kroo" and an occasional lower-pitched "kaak", which I found trickier to imitate. Almost twenty years ago now, I met a university biologist on the Canadian side of the border with Alaska, and he told me about ravens. He said a colleague had studied a group of them for many years and concluded that they have the widest vocabulary in all nature after human beings. He also found that every bird had one unique call that no other bird used. But when one bird died, all the others flew around for days using the unique call of the missing bird, as if they were looking for it, like a search party.

Armed with this knowledge, I often wonder when I talk back to ravens whether they have any idea what I'm saying. Obviously I have no idea what I'm saying. The raven on the dead tree flew suddenly, disappeared behind a screen of spruces. I turned back to my lunch, but seconds later I heard the rasp of wingbeats behind my back and spun round to see the raven swerve away from a flightpath that would have come very low over my head. Then it perched again on the top of a bare larch, this time about 150 yards away. The conversation resumed, and this time the raven's vocabulary was notably more varied. But it was suddenly restless and flew again, to a branch on a larch, which had been blown over but had snagged among its neighbours at an angle of about sixty degrees. It was now no more than fifty yards away, and once again the conversation resumed. How long all this might have lasted I will never know, because suddenly the far-off voice of a second raven sounded and everything changed. It arrived in a two-way chorus of non-stop raven voices and perched in a nearby larch. But the first raven flew again, and my guess is that this time it perched where it could watch us both at once.

I have no idea, of course, whether both ravens were including me in the conversation (for I continued to call).

I do know that they were holding a conversation and I was not. I left them to it. As I passed close to the first raven's tree I waved an arm and called loudly, a gesture that said, "Until the next time, and thanks for your company." I'm pretty sure it got the message.

◉ ◉ ◉

Two days later, back in the forest, following the path where I had chatted with the raven, the day too warm for early winter, for any kind of winter day, the mountain snow all too predictably reduced to streaks and patches. The only coldness was in the deep shadows of the spruces thrown by low sun. The path led to a new forest road that climbed to a high and heathery plateau well planted with young spruce and Scots pine. A wiser and more sensitive forestry design would have let the pines have their head here, so that its open character would be preserved. Heroic Scots pine would grow here, given the space which spruce plantation forestry routinely denies to anything else with slower-growing ambition. They would frame views to the mountains and create a wildlife habitat of exceptional richness, so typical of the right kind of Highland Edge landscapes which beckon to the tribes of both Highland and Lowland and invite them to co-exist. As it is, the nearest mountain (Ben Ledi at its most pyramidally striking) rose out of a dead-straight horizontal of spruce tops, and only two small copses of foreground Scots pines offered anything in the way of curves at all to soften the prospect.

A skinny little trail no wider than one of my boots led through heather towards a rocky knoll. On three bare patches, each of no more than a few square inches, I found the distinctive droppings of pine marten. At this moment in time, with the new woodland planting still in its infancy, give or take a handful of older pines (a sign of the old natural order before the foresters moved in), the spaciousness and the heather and the remnant scraps of the natural vegetation, the pine martens are thriving. But too much of it all will be lost to financial considerations which determine a preponderance of fast-growing spruces, and as these grow tall and bulk up into a dense and darkening overkill, the constituent elements of biodiversity simply move out or die off. There is a fine old Scots pine nearby, not tall but enthroned on space and broad-crowned. Twice in a previous spring I saw ospreys exploring here and alighting in the tree. It would seem to me to be a perfect osprey tree in a part of the country that sustains at least a dozen pairs (and a first principle of sound nature conservation is to safeguard strongholds and expand them wherever possible); then forestry operations began and the ospreys moved on.

⊙ ⊙ ⊙

Flanders Moss, a raised bog and a National Nature Reserve, in the last of the light. Ben Ledi had tugged a skullcap of flimsy brownish cloud across its summit. It looked perilously poised and several sizes too big, and leaned from east to west as though it had made an imperfect landing there. Every mountain in sight – Ben Vorlich, Stuc a' Chroin, Beinn Each, Ben Venue and Ben Lomond – was identically garbed in ill-fitting skullcaps and the ragged-edged look that comes from the too-fast melting of mountain snows into scattered patches that diminish by the hour. Tonight, what's left will freeze, and tomorrow, when the temperature rises and one more weak front of wet winds scuds in from the west, the rest will go. Welcome to the redefined nature of winter.

A string of five grazing roe deer inched slowly eastwards through the tall bleached-out grass immediately to the north of the Moss. There is a new high seat there for shooters; there are three now, each one more hideous than the others. The deer graze contemptuously close. I imagine they can tell when it's empty. The National Nature Reserve has an observation tower back against the birch wood that acts as a buffer between the south edge of the Moss and the flat fields of the Carse beyond. The observation platform on top is at treetop height, and to north, east and west, the view over the Moss is all-embracing, and terminates in that uncompromising arc of mountains. I spent some time studying fence posts and low trees in the binoculars, looking for hen harriers. There was a time when this was a nationally important winter roost site for harriers, but such has been their lurch towards extinction at the hands of so-called "sporting" estates, that nowhere can be judged nationally important now. Here, as in other traditional roosting sites, they just about cling on. If the bird on the fence post in the glasses is a gull-coloured male, he is easy enough to spot. If, however, it's a fence post-coloured female and she happens to be perched erect, what she looks like from a distance and in low light is a bit of fence post.

A flock of small birds sped through the glasses, and I refocused to follow them, a bouncing flock of tadpoles with straight tails. They flew past the top of the tower at eye level, and as they drew level with me they were side-on so that their wings "disappeared" against the silhouettes of their bodies, thus indulging the tadpole illusion. They were long-tailed tits, of course, and I expected them to settle into the tops of the birches, but they flew right through the topmost twigs and buds and carried on south. Did they know where they were going? It would be dark in half an hour and cold. Their long tails that so endear them to birdwatchers everywhere are a liability in winter, because they greatly extend the birds' surface areas and therefore their capacity to grow cold. They attempt to thwart the problem by roosting in a closely packed line along a branch, constantly changing places so that no bird is on the end of the line for too long. If winter continues to redefine itself along its chaotically warming path, the long-tailed tits at least might benefit.

On a parallel course to the vanished flock, but to my west rather than my east, a single raven approached, muttering to itself. It also flew through the treetops in its path without stopping. But almost at once, a second raven I had neither seen nor heard appeared, flying much higher. Its flightpath was so aligned that it appeared in the glasses against the out-of-focus bulk of Ben Ledi, so that as it flew I was conscious of the snow-patched, ridiculously skullcapped mountain massed immensely behind it, thus creating the illusion of an emissary despatched by the mountain. Perhaps Noah was up there, his ark perched on the summit inside the cloud, searching in vain not for dry land but for a semblance of winter.

This second raven perched in the top of a pine, also at my eye level from the top of the tower, and began calling vigorously, stretching his entire body, neck and head forward with each call, straining for volume and projection it seemed. There was a gap a second long between the mandibles opening to call and the sound reaching my ears, so that it looked like one of those television moments when sound and mouth are troublingly out of synch. Not for the first time in my life, or even in this first month of winter, I wished I was more fluent in the language of ravens.

⊙　⊙　⊙

My day often begins with a half-hour walk to get newspapers and coffee. I count bird species while I walk. My record, for what it's worth (which is nothing at all), is twenty-four. I am not, instinctively, a bird-counter. Nor do I keep records of numbers or dates. The interest as far as the morning walk is concerned stems from the small variations that occur within the familiar roll call. My antennae twitch at a snatch of an unfamiliar voice. On one of the very few frosty and misty journeys that December, there was hardly anything moving at all. Then one two-syllable call fell to earth and made my day. It was pitched somewhere between the woody voice of a clarinet and a muted flugelhorn, and it was high and somewhere over my right shoulder. I occasionally wonder if anyone watches me from behind net curtains at moments like this. I stopped dead, spun round, looked up, and eventually found a line-astern flight of five whooper swans, a family group of two adults and three of this year's cygnets, heading west. They came directly overhead, and about 200 feet up. I stayed still and staring until they had vanished over rooftops.

No day which starts that way can ever feel anything other than blessed. My debt to the wild swans of the north of the world is one that I can never adequately articulate, and as for repaying it, I wouldn't know how to begin. As it was, the brief incursion of the swans on my early morning acted on my mood like a fork of lightning out of a clear sky. Even the adults had looked grey in flight, for there was no sun and the mist dulled the sky, but I was dazzled by them. I felt as if they had sought me out, which is a preposterous notion once time has passed and you think back to it, but it always feels that way whenever my path crosses that of any one of the tribes of nature with which I feel a particular affinity. With swans, the pitch of that affinity is unique in my life, and I walked on with a headful of swans.

In particular, there was an old winter by a small hill lochan in the south of Skye, and another family of five whooper swans. I had heard them from some distance away, knew from former visits that they were on the lochan even before I could see it, so I approached with every nuance of stealth that I knew. I reached the nearest shore crawling with my chin in the peat, and just in time to see the cob rise up on the water and stand there, ankle deep. He had found a submerged rock, a favourite preening perch for swans everywhere. So he began to preen with only his feet and an inch or two of leg in the water. It was a less fluid routine than a mute swan, and I wondered whether the whooper's characteristically straighter neck is also a less flexible preening aid.

The pen was on the water and heading in his general direction but with her head deep in the feathers of her back and folded wings, preening as she swam. In that compacted pose she drifted directly in front of him. Sooner or later in any protracted preening routine, an adult swan stretches head and neck high, appears to "stand" on its tail, opens its wing-span to its full extent and beats its wings forcefully so that they sound like drying sheets in a big wind. At the precise moment when she reached him, he unfurled himself into that heroic pose. He was a particularly well-built cob, and when he opened his wings it was like the prelude to a vast embrace. For perhaps two seconds, the coiled form of his mate was canopied and quite dwarfed by the one wing beneath which she swam so obliviously, so furled beneath such a stupendous unfurling. Then she drifted on past him, reassembled herself into a swan shape, and swam off towards her brood at the far end of the lochan. He was simply a standing swan again, busy with his breast feathers.

The light began to drowse. I have much cause to be grateful to an instinct that urges me to linger through the last hour of half-light when there is little to see but the shifting mood of wildness as the laws of daylight peter out and the laws of darkness gather. I was still watching the swans when I became vaguely aware of a gentle splashing at my back where the lochan shore curved away from my limited field of vision. When it persisted and the swans started to react with stiffening necks and muttered calls and a slow advance a dozen yards across the lochan then a concerted discretionary halt, I eased my position as slowly as I could to look back over my left shoulder. Five red deer hinds and three calves had walked into the shallows fifty yards away, as unaware of me as I had been of them. I simply lay dead still, memorising everything.

They waded and drank and muttered. Red deer can be surprisingly vocal at close quarters and when the wind is in your favour. The swans, as far across the lochan in the other direction, paddled and fed and muttered. The deer voices were gruff, croaky, percussive. The swan voices were mellow, soft brass. Both sets of voices were couched in the speech of communication rather than concern. I wondered what Sibelius would have made of the hour.

Chapter Six

Whale Watch (1):
The Narwhal in the Sky

A STRANGE DAY DAWNED, a day autumn had stolen back from winter. En route for Glen Finglas, the Woodland Trust Scotland reserve and Ben Ledi's next door neighbour to the west, pausing on Loch Venachar's shore ... there, at noon, the day was *warm*, and so still that a hint of surrealism crept into the sunlit surface of the loch and the reflections of land and sky. There was no obvious join, no demarcation between reality and reflection, cloud and water seamlessly united, the western shore which includes Ben Venue was both suspended and afloat in sky and water simultaneously, neither the real land nor its reflection noticeably brighter or darker than the other, an equinox of the mind's eye. Was this autumn's revenge for winter gatecrashing autumn that day in the Pentland Hills? Do the seasons deal with each other that way? Is there a conversation, a negotiation, a deal, or just an uninvited raid, facilitated by one more foible of the jetstream?

The Glen Finglas oakwood was deep dark brown, mysteriously suntanned. All the leaves had turned, but they still clung to the trees in huge quantities. By early December

2015, four of those storms the Met Office likes to refer to by their Christian names (Abigail to Desmond) had already bludgeoned the trees bare and left quite a few of them prostrate on the forest floors of the land. But by early December 2016, the back end of the year had been utterly stormless. The result was an atmosphere within the oakwood of otherworldly tranquillity, as if the natural order of things had been suspended, as if time itself had been outwitted. The oakleaves had passed through all the phases of photosynthesis demanded of them by nature except the final one. Once the leaves stop producing chlorophyll, its green signature is replaced by a yellow one (carotenoid) or a red one (anthocyanin) or both, and when these fade, decomposed carbohydrates and oxidised tannins turn the leaves brown. Then the autumn gales invade the woods and the leaves are blown off. But there had been no wind, even by December, and the leaves still clung, but lifelessly; brown shrouds in a brown mortuary.

Sunlight was the saving grace of the place that day, for it lit and shadowed all that brown-ness. When a female buzzard and I surprised each other (she had her back to me and the sun, using it to spotlight fugitive prey by positioning herself on an oak limb so that the light came over her shoulder), she parted with the tree in such a way that it was as if a fragment of the oakwood cloak had been prised away from the whole and unwillingly cast adrift. For she flew so knowingly through that web of trunk and twig and branch and limb, and she bore in her plumage – and especially in the fluctuating revelations of upper and lower wings – every single shade of the winter oak; she was as much of the wood as every living tree and every fallen tree. The sense that my arrival in the wood had wounded some ancient peace lingered with me until I climbed up beyond the highest oaks and out into the more open-handed generosity of the embryonic birch wood above, then the broad expanses of mountainside with their splashes of tall, slender pines against the skyline.

These are survivors from the commercial forestry that predated Woodland Trust Scotland's benevolent rescue operation. The dense spruce was felled, birch and pine enclaves had somehow found a niche and with no room to fill out they survived by putting all their energies into growing tall. They may not look much, but they are seed-bearers and they beget more of their kin, and that is the object of the exercise.

I paused – as I always do – at the bench dedicated to the memory of one William Butler. I know nothing about him, but I refer to him as Yeats, for obvious reasons. Sometimes I speak Yeats to him, such as *He Wishes for the Cloths of Heaven* or this one-verse poem entitled *The Coming of Wisdom with Time*, which strikes me as a fitting epitaph for a woodland memorial:

Though leaves are many, the root is one;
Through all the lying days of my youth
I swayed my leaves and flowers in the sun;
Now I may wither into the truth.

The bench faces the sun with a wide view of the loch far below, and beyond that the distant wooded slopes of Achray Forest. These, along with Glen Finglas and other woodlands all the way west to Loch Lomond, comprise the Great Trossachs Forest, a 21st-century conservation endeavour of great promise. I like to sit and write there. On that December day of unseasonal warmth and calm I listened to far-carrying sounds: a dog bark at a distant farm, the woodwind sigh of bullfinches, and the one that made me wish I could spin my head through 180 degrees like an owl – the high-pitched, incongruous yet unmistakable terrier yap of a golden eagle. I found it in the glasses eventually, much higher than I had thought it should be and almost directly overhead. It was the fourth time I had seen an eagle from that seat in two years; one more reason why William Butler's thoughtfully-placed memorial endears itself to me, likewise his family who thought fit to put it there.

I watched the eagle climb out of sight (it simply became too tiny), but the arrival of the sound of its voice in my ear, fallen to earth like a discarded feather, had only been possible because of the stillness of the day, the clarity of the air, and the fact that whenever I am alone in wild places, I am increasingly intrigued by that idea I have mentioned before of *listening* to the land. It is the simplest of ideas and one of the oldest; it is the basis of a relationship with landscape common to many of the native peoples of the northern hemisphere.

You make a space in the day. You think only about listening. You give it time. Those are the essentials. Slowly, you can begin to reach beyond the surface sounds and detect the presence of something beyond them, something deeper. Then your eyes begin to assist the process of listening.

So, there was a moment within that hour of profound calm when every shallow curve and every deeper breast-shaped curve in the contours of the wooded hillside below became a kind of breathing, the breathing of the land itself, and there is at least the sense of something other: the speech that flows between land and forest and water emerged as a conversation on which I could eavesdrop. The American nature writer Barry Lopez hinted at something similar when he wrote of a conversation he had with an old Eskimo woman about a visual equivalent of that "something other" in his book *Arctic Dreams* (Scribner's, 1986), then interpreted it thus:

> *To put it another way, occasionally one sees something fleeting in the land, a moment when line, colour and movement intensify and something sacred is revealed, leading one to believe that there is another realm of reality corresponding to the physical one but different ...*

George Garson would have nodded his head agreeably at that. I subscribe to it wholeheartedly.

I felt embraced by the moment. I had become a fragment of the land. It is the highest and most elusive ideal I can strive for as a nature writer, a condition which feels as if I can respond to the land with animal sensitivity. I have proved to myself over and over again that nature's most elusive qualities and secrets come within reach when you can let them come to you. Stillness is the key to all of it. Can you be still enough for long enough to become a part of the landscape in nature's eyes? Almost always, some mundane intrusion from the world beyond its force-field ends it. This time, it was the crescendo throb of a helicopter. But briefly, I lingered in that other realm of reality corresponding to the physical one but different. And long after the helicopter had come and gone and its engine notes absorbed back into the world of uncountable engine notes, the eagle voice came back to me and I was able to recreate its potency, its other-world-ness, its wildness; it is, if you have ears to hear it, the very speech of nature, the language of the world as defined by nature.

I turned my attention back to the hillside below. I love the pines at this time of year, when every other tree is either brown or bare or both. They appear to glow, as if they are lit from within. That particular winter circumstance of dead calm (wrong expression – *living* calm), the air rinsed clean, the land lit by the afternoon sun low in the south-west…all that conspired to show off the finery of pines while every other tree on the hillside was smoored. At its most exhibitionistic, the phenomenon alighted on a small heathery knoll where two pines have flourished spectacularly in the dozen years of their liberation from that old spruce stranglehold. One is twice the height of the other, but the other has twice the spread. The trunk of the taller tree forked about six feet off the ground, in order to send two perfectly parallel limbs shooting skywards, so that now it brandishes its double crown forty feet above its roots. I have seen many pine trees I would call handsome, but I have never seen another one with quite this elegance. And here was a day designed by this showiest of winter moods to show it off as I and that high-flying eagle (which will know it for a landmark, as I do myself, and must surely have perched there) had never seen it before.

In the late afternoon, with the sun half in and half out of that realm of shadows beyond the hills in the south-west, I felt the air stir and knew it at once for the breath of winter. Then the air went immediately cold. One hour hence, it would be deep dusk and deep winter cold, the day's illusion done. It would prove to be the first of many illusions in which this particularly skittish winter would indulge itself. Global warming's southwards seepage down through the northern hemisphere from the Arctic is making mockeries of the very nature of winter itself. But for now, I watched a thin, creeping, purplish band of cloud begin to wrap itself across the half-sunk sun. Its progress across the sky held an indefinably ominous air and made for hypnotic watching. When I eventually turned my back on it, I was just in time to see my shadow fade into the hillside. At once, the cold rushed in around my neck. Then, there was that sacred thing again, a force of such quietness that I was compelled to linger and listen to its symphonic purity. My stillness felt like a kind of command. No nature writer worth the name is deaf or disobedient to nature's commands. It could have been moments or minutes or half an hour.

It ended in uncontrollable, spell-breaking shivers. The unmistakable rasp of a dog fox snapped up out of the woods below me, a harsh discordancy, but one more pointed utterance in nature's vocabulary. I turned away downhill to consider all that I had just heard.

◎ ◎ ◎

Sometimes I think I believe in omens. If that sounds half-hearted, that's because it is, because a belief in omens is a tough creed to commit to, because by the very unchancy nature of their appearance, they invite doubt, scorn, disbelief. What, for example, am I supposed to make of a whale that was about to appear in the sky?

I had just shared that landscape's brief era of quietude with eagle and fox, vivid embellishments to the day's tapestry of nature's moods from lochside to oakwood to open hill. I was already thrilled by a kind of lingering unease before that eerie cloud ushered the sun from the sky, and I watched the western sky as I dropped back down the hillside. It was then that a new cloud shape materialised above Ben Venue, the mountain which dominates the very heart of the Trossachs, and this one stopped me dead. It was the shape of a narwhal, complete with long, slender, tapering tusk, jutting out dead straight from its head. I stared and stared and stared. If I concede that the moment was attended by a sense of omen, I should also acknowledge that I was clueless about what kind of message it might be trying to impart. It is a long, long way from the landlocked Trossachs of the Scottish Highlands' most southerly mountains to the Arctic Ocean domain of the narwhal.

The narwhal is a kind of wolf of Arctic waters, if only in the sense that humanity has endowed it with bizarre legend and misunderstanding fuelled by ignorance of what it is and what it does. Stir into the brew of centuries the unicornish connotations of the tusk, and the narwhal has offered up one of the most fertile sources of legend-making ever to spew forth from some of the most irrational excesses of human imagination. It is comparatively recently that any reliable information at all began to emerge about where narwhals go and what they do in winter, and that has only been possible because of global warming, because the disappearance of Arctic sea ice has become as much of a threat to the very existence of the narwhal as it is to the polar bear.

Among the things we still don't know is the origin of its name, and there seem to be almost as many theories out there as there are whales in the oceans. One of the oldest and most persistent centres around a theme of death, apparently because its pallid skin is thought to resemble that of a human corpse. Old ones have been known to turn quite white. In some circumpolar societies, its appearance was an omen, and thought to presage a human death; or it became symbolic of human death. Happily, I was still unaware of this when my own narwhal omen loomed above its mountaintop.

And then there is the question of the tusk. What is it for? It is, almost exclusively, the preserve of the males, but it is not a weapon. They don't impale their prey on it (they catch fish, notably cod and halibut, in their mouths), they don't wound rival males with it, or fend off attacks from their predators, the killer whales and the polar bears.

It is, in reality, a tooth, their only tooth. It is one continuous spiral and crammed with nerve ends, and it appears to pierce the upper lip on the left side of the narwhal's head. Two males will sometimes cross tusks, like swords, but there is no clear evidence that it is a ritual pose with a purpose, or whether it is even a deliberate manoeuvre. One of the more persuasive possibilities is that in narwhal mating society, size matters, that the bigger the tusk, the more dominant the animal, the more impressed are the females. Some biologists make comparisons with a stag's antlers. God knows why.

The narwhal is one of the smaller whales. It can grow to about sixteen feet, but its girth can be eight feet and it can weigh two tons. Add on ten feet of tusk and you have a considerable presence. They can also dive to improbable depths, although science differs with itself about just how deep. Half a mile, perhaps. Its unique underwater life, and especially its under-ice life, is where the waters really start to muddy.

But when one appeared in a Highland sky to adorn a winter sunset, the effect was magical. The tusk extended levelly across the sky, tapering, to end in a perfect point above the sunken sun, so that it was tipped with gold. The head of the narwhal cloud flamed briefly, while its underside beneath the tail echoed that shade more palely, a gentler flame. I had never seen a cloud like that before, so I took some photographs, unaware for the moment that right then and a few thousand miles to the north-west, one more symptom of global warming had just dumped a new and life-threatening crisis on the narwhal's distinguished head, and then there was the coincidence of what followed. The particular nature of what a Highland winter has become, a disjointed series of the briefest fragments of snowy and frosty weather punctuating long and turgid swathes of mild grey gloom, and of which the winter of 2016–17 would prove to be the most convincing example yet, is global warming writ large and indelibly. Believe in it.

If you have been writing about nature for a living for thirty years, and studying it for rather longer, your perspective is arguably as valid as anyone's. If you weigh the verdict of those sources you trust among the world's biologists, ecologists and nature writers of, say, the last 200 years, then set that in the context of what you have seen and questioned for yourself, then there is only one reasonable conclusion. It is that global warming is no longer a disaster waiting to happen – it has begun, it is already happening, and it is travelling with terrifying speed towards the point beyond which it will not be reversible. Right now, I think that winter itself may be halfway towards extinction, that the wild year will soon be measurable in three seasons – a spring that lasts from February to May, summer from June to September, and autumn from October to January. There will be savours of those winters of memory from time to time, but they will be fragments that conjure up little more than nostalgia. We would get the storms, the fleeting shades of the season formerly known as winter, but no more seasons of sustained snow and ice, no more weeks at a time of a land locked up in sub-zero temperatures. In winter's place there has emerged a troublesome species of climate chaos. And the idea of four seasons will be reduced to a piece of music by Vivaldi.

Which brings me back to the plight of the narwhal. The narwhal is an Arctic specialist. Unlike many whale species, it doesn't migrate to warmer waters, but remains in Arctic waters all year where it can live under the sea ice. At the time the narwhal-shaped cloud appeared in the Trossachs sky, and quite unknown to me then, narwhal on the north coast of Canada's Baffin Island were having a specific problem. That problem was killer whales. But the reason they were having a problem with killer whales at all is global warming. In February 2017, the Canadian Department of Fisheries and Oceans published the find-ings of their study of the narwhal's particular problem. The presence of killer whales, said the study, "is intimidating the narwhal into drastically altered behaviour. It's another symptom of how climate change is remaking the delicate northern environment."

Most narwhal "overwinter" (if I am right about the near future, we are going to have to find a new verb for that idea soon) for up to five months under sea ice around Baffin Bay and Davis Strait. But 5,000 of them spend the summer in Admiralty Inlet on the north coast of Baffin Island and 500 miles north of the Arctic Circle. There, they have been accustomed to enjoy the protection of sea ice. Crucially, as far as the narwhal are concerned, killer whales don't like sea ice, so their presence in these, the narwhal's calving grounds, had always been limited. But the rapid decline of the summer sea ice means that the narwhal are much more accessible. So the killer whales have started to arrive in greater numbers, arrive earlier and stay longer.

"Inlet" is a deceptive word in the circumstances, inviting thoughts of tranquillity and landscape intimacy. Admiralty Inlet is huge – almost 200 miles long and thirty wide. Historically, the narwhal hunted between two and six miles offshore. But now, whenever the killers are present anywhere at all in the inlet, the narwhal "cower" (the revealing word used by the Canadian study) within 500 yards of the shore. They have a unique system of communication between groups which spreads the word of the killers' presence several miles out to sea, so they cower inshore, and they become easy pickings in what had always been one of the richest and safest of hunting grounds. One of the study report's authors said that "the narwhal are scared to death". Then he offered this chilling thought:

*Most traditional science views changes from the bottom up
– the food supply changes and it ripples its way up the food
chain. A few of us believe the changes can happen from the top
down and be just as significant.*

As in nature, so in politics: changes can happen from the top
down and be just as significant, witness the behaviour of the
Trump administration in Washington.

It is hard to overstate the significance of Arctic sea ice in
terms of nature's own ideas about what constitutes a healthy
planet. The ice's underside is densely coated with algae, the
essential original source of a chain reaction that reverber-
ates out into the oceanic world. These feed zooplankton,
unimaginably large clouds of which drift through the upper
layers of the sea. They are, in turn, devoured in unimaginably
large quantities by fish like cod. The fish feed seabirds and
narwhal, and the ringed seals that feed the polar bears and
(once the bears have had their fill) the Arctic foxes. Ice binds
all this together. Ice-thirled seals, like the ringed seals, are
not comfortable hauled out on a beach; they are vulnerable
there. But out on the ice they can rest up directly above their
feeding grounds. And ice is where they have their pups. And
ice is also how the bears reach the seals.

Narwhal seem to be able to read the ice like no other
creature in the Arctic Ocean. When a "lead" (a channel of
temporarily open water in an ice field) is about to close,
trapping them under an extent of ice too long for them to
travel on a single breath, they sense the advent of the change
and they leave. This kind of specialised sensitivity to their

ice world is also communicated around different groups of narwhal by methods that are still not completely understood. Scientists have talked of tape recordings of narwhal being "saturated" with the tumult of their acoustic emissions.

Such intuitive genius is not lost on this Scottish nature writer, observing in some detail the nature of this winter of 2016–17 in his own part of the world and finding it bestrewn with admittedly smaller symptoms of the chaotic phenomenon that is climate change. But it bears repeating what John Muir knew 120 years ago when he was writing *My First Summer in the Sierra*:

When we try to pick out anything by itself we find it hitched to everything else in the Universe.

We know that too, of course, but we forget we know it, or we choose to ignore that we know it, and then the facts get in the way and we remember again, when it's too late. Satellite records from America's National Snow and Ice Data Center showed that in February 2017, the extent of Arctic sea ice averaged 5.51 million square miles, "the lowest February extent in the 38-year satellite record", and 15,400 square miles less than 2016. The summer sea ice of 2016 reached a "statistical tie" for the second lowest Arctic sea ice minimum at 1.6 million square miles, and only 290,000 square miles more than the record low point in 2012. If these numbers sound comfortingly large to you, then consider this: in the first thirty-eight years of these records, two million square miles of midwinter sea ice simply disappeared – two million and counting. And how far away can we possibly be before the Arctic summer sea ice disappears altogether? And, because "when we try to pick out anything by itself we find it hitched to everything else in the Universe", it stands to reason that the consequences will be far-reaching.

Some more numbers for you to consider, courtesy of my Alaskan friend, the writer and teacher Nancy Lord, in her book *Early Warming* (Counterpoint, 2011):

> *I know these numbers: White sea ice reflects about eighty per cent of the sun's heat, blue water absorbs ninety per cent.*
>
> *And these: Twenty years ago, eighty per cent of Arctic ice was at least ten years old; in 2007 only three per cent was that old.*
>
> *And this fact: The Arctic has been ice-free in summer before, but, according to the National Snow and Ice Data Center, scientists have confidence that the last time was 125,000 years ago ...*

The melting of the polar ice sheets may be seen as a kind of global shorthand for climate change at work, but I can perhaps be forgiven for wondering what nature was up to when it grafted a narwhal onto a Trossachs skyline.

Chapter Seven

Solstice

THE YEAR DWINED towards midwinter. The sun had been a fleeting, pale-faced stranger in the hills, the snow when it came was deep and wet high up, but the temperature never stayed low enough for long enough to stabilise it, so it leaked water by the ton into dark gullies wrapped in long, skinny and restless fragments of cloud that drifted and reshaped and disintegrated before a cold, clammy, listless wind. One morning, the mountainside was striped with white-foaming burns, hoarse and loud-mouthed. They charged down the gullies, rain hissed on the bent and broken tea-stained leaves of withered ferns and heather. In forty-eight hours, all that had eased down to a dripping, listless day of uneasy calm.

There is rowan up there on that Glen Dochart mountainside which cleaves to a buttress, a skinny little runt of a tree going nowhere, especially not upwards. Yet it has clawed sustenance there for thirty years that I know of, and quite possibly for twice that long. Whoever came up with the adage "you can't get blood out of a stone", never reckoned with the raw tenacity of a mountainside rowan. I have seen a golden eagle pluck a sprig from it in its green portion of the year, for all that it is fully a mile from the rowan's buttress to the eagle eyrie buttress.

And there I sat, holding a one-sided *ceilidh* with the rowan, huddled under an overhang, hands clamped on the cup of my flask, drinking two-handed while the coffee still steamed, and happed in ridiculously expensive waterproofs and boots; and still the sodden air found a way inside the jacket's neck and hood the way spiders and slaters suddenly turn up mysteriously in your bath, as I explained it to the rowan. You can dress for weather like this, but that does not necessarily mean you can keep it out.

But sometimes it is simply part of the job, and the bizarre truth is that I was enjoying myself. There is a perverse satisfaction sitting on a familiar mountainside when most of the views are down and none of them are long, as secure on my chosen cleft of rock as that rowan, friend of the wind and the rain and fellow traveller of the snows, and intimate companion of the mountain itself.

"Intimate" is the essential word for a nature writer. It's why I work a particular landscape the way an eagle works a territory. And intimacy with a landscape, with how nature works in that landscape, is gleaned from a day like this as much as from a blue, shirt-sleeve day of late spring clarity and endless sightlines, of ring ousel song and a litter of orchids in long summer grass. I need them all, and I need to know how they are connected. My Alaskan writer-friend Nancy Lord wrote in a beautiful book of essays called *Rock, Water, Wild – An Alaskan Life* (University of Nebraska Press, 2009), "I learned to pay attention, the most essential writer's work". I read that and I thought: "Comrade!" So there I sat in the dripping snowscape, conversing with a rock-rooted rowan and paying attention, and I felt well attuned to the hour and the day, waiting for something to turn up, and five red deer hinds and three calves had just filed out of a slaister of screes and boulders a hundred feet below me, out into what on a better day you might call "the open".

I hadn't seen them coming. But there again, on such a day with no long sightlines in any direction, unplanned encounters like this one were very much part of the plan. Sometimes, just being there is all that matters, and you let the day take care of itself.

The deer were as unaware of me as I had been of them until a few seconds ago, but right now they were movement and I was stillness, so for the moment I had an edge. With luck, and if no unkindly wind sprung up, things might stay that way for a while.

They walked slowly and in single file, a trail-breaking matriarch with three younger animals directly behind her, then the calves and a grey-faced old veteran bringing up the rear. The snow was old, wet and deep, and I had stumbled knee-deep more than once on my way up. But I noticed the matriarch had chosen a contour where the snow was no more than three or four inches deep. So there is the kind of intimacy that *I* feel for this mountainside, and then there is the intimacy a mature red deer hind brings to bear on every living, breathing moment, so that it extends to the way the snow lies on any particular slope, the ledges where it deepens beyond what is comfortable, and the flat-topped bluffs and buttresses where the work of a particular wind from a particular airt over a particular number of days thins the snow to a workable shallowness. She reads and understands her mountain the way you or I might read and understand this page of this book. She is fluent in its language.

She angled up the near flank of a buttress directly below me, and where I had expected to see her struggle in deep drifts, she had found a runnel of water that oozed from the base of the buttress, and she stepped elegantly up there on almost bare rock. The younger hinds had stopped at the base and watched her for a few seconds. If I was inclined towards anthropomorphism, I would say that when they followed they did so with admiration and gratitude – but I don't care too much for anthropomorphism, so I will concede only that the gratitude and admiration were all mine.

On the top of the buttress she stopped and began pawing the snow until she bared a few square inches of mountain grasses, mosses and lichens, then she lowered her head to eat. The others went to work after the same fashion. The snow there was no more than two inches deep.

But where was the old one? She had not made the climb up the flank of the buttress. I took a long look down what I could see of their tracks back to the boulderfield, and of the wide slope below. So I was not looking at the deer at the precise moment when her grey head would have appeared from below and beyond the far side of the buttress. When I did look back at the deer she was already there, pawing the snow and feeding with the rest. Much later, once they had taken all that they could from the meagre offerings of the buttress-top (in a moment I was handed a vivid new definition of the expression "slim pickings", and these were on the skinny side of slim), I dropped below the buttress to look at the old one's tracks.

They were not hard to find. She had passed beneath the buttress and contoured about fifty yards beyond it, to where a venerable stalker's path zigged and zagged easy gradients into the slope, and where days-old boot prints had stamped the snow into a red deer walkway as flat and firm as bare rock. Intimacy, you see? That's what it looks like through her eyes.

I have a notion of my own that the hind which led the way up there had learned about the bite of old grass under the snow above the buttress from the old grey-faced one. When the deer finally moved on, they descended by the old one's route and resumed their original contour line and disappeared by degrees into the gloom. If they had registered my presence at all, they gave no hint of it.

I moved off downhill, for I didn't much care for the look of the sky in the north-east, and took easy slopes above the gully of a burn that slithered quietly away to the distant river. I was still thinking about the deer and what it must be like to carry that kind of map of the mountain in your head, when I heard voices from below, thin and high-pitched and just about carrying above the voice of the burn. From the edge of the gully the source was obvious at once – snow buntings again, a flock of about thirty, every one of them clinging to the swaying tops of the bleached hill grass that grew thickly in a sheltered corner of the bank of the burn, every one of them plundering seeds, and flickering palely in short flights from one grass stem to another, the air as vibrant with the white flash of wings and tails as with their voices.

Snow buntings are among the boldest of small birds, so I took a chance and simply sat down on the top of the bank a dozen yards away and watched. Once again, not one reacted to my presence. They were nearly all males, which is the norm for a winter mountain flock. Science thinks they are better insulated than the females and first-year birds, which tend to winter in Scotland around the coasts, and it seems as likely an explanation as any.

Eight red deer and thirty snow buntings. If anything else at all moved on that mountainside in the four hours I was out there, they left neither sight nor sound of their passage. The most compelling characteristic of the day was its utter quietness, a few soft mutterings from the deer, the thin havers of the birds, a half-hearted wind, a soft-voiced burn; not so much as a raven croak to disturb the equilibrium of late afternoon. The buntings were still there when I stood and left, still swinging and swaying with the wind and the tall grass.

In the night it snowed hard on the mountain. Eight red deer, thirty snow buntings and a rowan tree rooted in rock all tholed a night such as you and I can barely imagine; the deer and the birds finding shelter of a kind, the rowan leaning out from the rock into the storm like the bowsprit of the *Discovery* in her Arctic-going prime. The snow buntings would fly on and head for lower ground if things became too rough on the mountain. But the long winter of the red deer had only just begun.

⊙ ⊙ ⊙

One watershed to the south of the rowan tree's buttress, the River Balvaig eases itself gently through the mouth of Balquhidder Glen, performs a right turn, and heads south for Loch Lubnaig. The Gaelic word *Lub* means a "bend", and Loch Lubnaig is roughly boomerang-shaped, or at least the particular fold in the hills where it lies is boomerang-shaped. The popular tourist-fodder derivation of the name is the "crooked" loch, but I don't buy into tourism fodder too eagerly. There are any number of curved or bent or kinked or otherwise misshapen lochs all over Scotland, and none of them has a name that approximates to crooked loch, and Loch Lubnaig's gentle curve is too unexceptional to explain the name. On the other hand, its most distinguishing feature occurs where the Balvaig thrusts an exuberant entrance into its northern shore, creating a kind of watery avenue by virtue of an extravagant extension of its tree-lined banks well out into the loch. The effect is to create two distinctive bays, and one of the Gaelic words for a bay is *Luib*. Hence Lubnaig. That at least is what makes sense to me.

I have known this loch now for forty years. If that tract of Highland Edge country I think of as my nature writer's territory were a single living organism, Loch Lubnaig would be its beating heart. For ten of those forty years I lived within two miles of it, at the mouth of Balquhidder Glen, but even before I moved my writing life there I knew the loch intimately, for I had long been accustomed to travelling there from Stirling on a regular basis. I placed a high value on the creative energy I drew from crossing that landscape frontier, that Highland Edge, from the last of the fields through the foothills and into the first of the mountains. That sense of frontier was most tellingly articulated in winter. First snow on the mountains while Stirling still lazed in its own mild micro-climate acted on me like a summons. So did second snow, for that matter, and third, all the way through to the last snows of early spring. I remember the first time as vividly as I remember the most recent. The sense of being inhaled by the mountains has never left me. Likewise the sense of Ben Ledi as a kind of lynchpin, or a fulcrum, of all Scotland. I like to think that the earliest settlers in the flat-bottomed Carse of Stirling would treat its defining presence on their northern skyline as something sacred, a fit abode for the mountain gods to which they adhered. It is a cold soul who is indifferent to such surroundings.

Into the swamp of mild, dark grey days that heaped up one on top of the other as December of 2016 sauntered towards the solstice, nature suddenly whipped up a hard frost and a gentle but ice-tinged wind. I am not sure what it says about my character, but I could have skipped with gratitude. That same morning, the waxwings arrived and clustered in the topmost bare branches of a conspicuous birch not far from my house. Year after year – if they come at all – they end up sooner or later on that tree, either forgetful of or indifferent to the fact that every year the neighbourhood sparrowhawks have been waiting and watching for them. Walking between the front door of the house and the car about ten yards away, I saw them reintroduce themselves to each other in the time-honoured fashion – the hawk's low-level sprint up the grown-over course of a hidden burn then the soaring, thrilling power-climb up through the branches of the tree, followed by a cloudburst of waxwings.

The hawk dived hard left and the denouement was hidden from view by shrubbery. At least one of winter's characteristic rituals had slipped into place. I drove cheerfully north for the loch, hoping against hope that frost and the resumption of hawk-waxwing hostilities amounted to a good omen. Sometimes, the nature-writing life tiptoes into some of the mind's stranger backwaters.

The journey crept under Ben Ledi through the Pass of Leny (the first and last thoroughfare of the Highlands for millions of travellers over thousands of years), its dark, tumbling waters shaded by rearing, forested hillsides. Long before the A84 threaded its tight turns, it must have been the kind of place to give travellers pause for thought. Lowlanders straying this way for the first time must have feared for their lives. It is still one of the most dramatic landscape transformations in the country because one side is Lowland and the other instant and full-on Highland. It still comes as something of a shock to the system for first-time travellers from the south, following the gentle course of the A84 between Stirling and Callander, and then the sudden realisation in Callander that there is a mountain apparently at the end of the main street.

The quiet west side of Loch Lubnaig is tucked right in under that very mountain, just yards from the hem of Ben Ledi's skirts. I paused to look for signs of beavers along the River Leny. There have already been a couple of expeditionary sallies this way, and there is the beginning of what should prove to be a more settled presence a little further north. These are the explorers from the Tayside population. They crossed a single watershed from Loch Earn, probably by way of Glen Ample under the joined-at-the-hip mountains of Stuc a' Chroin and Ben Vorlich, and that was enough to bring them into the upper reaches of the Forth river system, with hundreds of miles of new beaver territory to colonise. The wonderfully wooded Trossachs area awaits their arrival with longing, their return after an absence of rather more than 300 years.

Deep and dark grey cloud hung about the mountains' waists on both sides of the loch. The unseen summits and ridges somehow contrived to insinuate themselves as a *presence*. But none had quite the aura of Ben Ledi itself, whose height was utterly unguessable from the depths of its frosted shadow. The lowest slopes wore a crust of dark, bare oaks, some of them of great age, a hint of how the land might have looked before all this became the fiefdom of the Forestry Commission's Strathyre Forest. Above and beyond the oaks, reaching into the clouds, a cloak of the Commission's default species, Sitka spruce, smouldered and shivered. Patches of birch and swathes of larch lightened the mountain's tree burden, and across the loch, there were outcrops of Scots pine. I do not share the widespread conservation view that the Sitka spruce is public enemy number one. It is not the tree's fault that it fell into the hands of monoculturalists. It bears repeating that it is a handsome tree that suits the Highland landscape well enough, and demonstrably it thrives here. A little more enlightenment in how the forestry industry deploys it would go a long way towards improving the ecology and biodiversity of the Highlands. I am fortunate to have been to Sitka, in south-east Alaska, and seen the temperate rainforest there, where the spruces are the basis of a phenomenal wild forest in the company of hemlock, aspen, birch, willow, and all that sustains wolf packs, bears, wolverines, beavers, bald eagle nests every half mile or so, and a great deal more besides. Should we be doing more to expand, enhance, recreate and restore native woodland cover? Yes, of course we should. Should we also accept the Sitka spruce as part of the mix, given that it has been with us since David Douglas, the son of a Perthshire stonemason, brought it back from North America the better part of 200 years ago? Yes, of course we should.

Right here, right now, the best of the spruce-dominated forests also accommodate larch and Scots pine, aspen, alder, willow, rowan and a great deal of birch; and these give homes to red squirrels, red and roe deer, red fox, pine martens, beavers, otters and a mix of birds ranging in size from gold-crests and wrens to ospreys and sea eagles.

In the deep stillness of that frosted morning, the voice of a raven rebounded off the rocks of the pass, so that it responded to its own echo, mixing up the calls from its impressive vocabulary in a kind of vocal perpetual motion. I wondered whether it had fooled itself into thinking it was addressing another bird, or whether it understood the concept of an echo completely and had a favourite rock where it was accustomed to perch and sing to the mountain, which answered it back with its echo, just like Sparky. I tend towards some version of the latter, because ravens are smart and work things out. Ravens are a constant four-season presence in this landscape, but they seem to have evolved a much more successful strategy for surviving a Highland winter's lean times than many of their wild fellow travellers.

The voice stopped. The echo stopped. There was a creaking rasp of wings. The raven flew directly over my head, looking down, drawn it would seem towards the only moving creature that shared its portion of the morning.

It circled twice, the blackest of black birds, darkened still further by the mountain massed behind it. Then it banked and flew away low across the surface of the loch's south end, where its reflection glided upside-down through the still water, matching the bird's downstroke with an upstroke, and vice-versa, a vaguely hypnotic progress.

Just where the loch gave way to the river, just where an alder branch bowed low towards the instantly white and turbulent water before it curved back upwards a yard into the air ... just at the lowest dip of the branch and inches above the spray, there emerged a new and weirdly out-of-season sound: birdsong at the winter solstice. Weirdly out-of-season, that is, if you don't know about dippers. There is no season of the year, no intensity of cold, no lash of wind or weight of downpour, no blizzard, no fog, nor dazzle of midwinter sun ... none of these things can stifle the male dipper's desire to sing.

Tiny icicles hung from the very branch where he stood and sang, icicles formed from the splashed spray of the river. The dark browns of the bird, relieved by the tiny white patch of his breast feathers, and the massed greys of the trees and the bank behind him, the greys and browns and white froth of the river, all conspired to set off the silver brilliance of his thin scatter of notes. It would hardly have surprised me to see them freeze in mid-air and drop into the river with minute silver splashes. Instead, the singing stopped abruptly, and the dipper tipped forward into a six-inch dive and vanished underwater. He appeared a few seconds later over by the far bank, swam a yard through shallow water, stepped onto a rock and proceeded to bash the living daylights out of a tiny silver fish by hitting its head against the rock. Kingfishers use the same technique, but they don't introduce the killing with song. The dipper re-crossed the river towards a conspicuously pyramid-shaped rock. He hit the water a yard from the rock then travelled towards it more or less by walking on water, which is neither as difficult nor as unusual as it sounds if you have the dipper's more or less limitless repertoire of amphibious techniques at your disposal. I watched him fish. The immersions often seemed longer than can possibly be good for him. After a dozen forays into the river, he suddenly changed tack, flew from the rock in a tight circle to where a natural bankside canal slightly higher than the mainstream ended in a tiny waterfall which, until moments before, had been behind the dipper's back whenever it perched on the rock. What changed? Was he mysteriously alerted to the presence of prey there (sound? eyes in the back of his head?), or is the bird's knowledge of its territory so intimate that he knew the small ledge above and behind the pyramid rock was always worth exploring? Whatever the reason, he caught and despatched several tiny fish within a few minutes.

Further up the loch, the north wind picked up and added its chill factor to the morning. Out in the middle of the middle, where I imagine the wind was flourishing at the peak of its powers, a single cormorant was flying head-on to the blast and just above the small waves which had mustered there. It landed abruptly, executed something like a forward roll that took it clear of the water in a curve, then dived deep. Nature, I decided, deals differently with the cold than I do. After two more miles of lochside, I turned uphill and into the forest for a respite from the wind and for lunch. It was like stepping into a hobbit-hole, and as you know, that means comfort.

The wind was instantly snuffed out, there was no frost, I was in a tiny clearing among oaks, the oaks themselves encircled on three sides by spruces. The fourth side was the steep bank I had just climbed, and so close were the oaks at the top of it that there was no view out to the loch or the sky at all. I sat on a small level ledge, sumptuously padded with moss. Closer inspection revealed that it was part of a fallen tree trunk. The gathering of oaks was defined to north and south by two tiny burns, whose voices added to the aura of comfort and something suspiciously like warmth.

Every woodland has these secret places, although in truth they are only "secret" to travellers like you and me, for they are frequented daily by many a forest dweller. Bullfinch, jay, wren, chaffinch and red squirrel all visited during the hour I spent there, sitting still and looking round, eating a sandwich and drinking hot tea. By one of the burns I could see where both badger and roe deer had paused to drink and dig.

I also puzzled over an oak tree with seven trunks, for no other reason than that it was the most conspicuous object in my line of sight without turning round. One trunk was straight and erect and much thicker (a girth of about five feet) than the rest. The others all leaned away from it at various angles and in every direction. I reconstructed the tree's life in my mind as follows:

The single trunk prospered in a mild corner of the forest, shielded from every wind, its soil drained by the two burns and enriched by leaf-litter and moss. When it produced its acorns, these simply fell below its own canopy because there was no wind to scatter them. Jay and squirrel buried some where they fell. The moss that gathers in deep, dense, lime green cushions around the base of such an oak tree also absorbed some and these rooted eventually in the same soil as the parent tree. As these developed as new trunks, the naturally expanding girth of their parent tree fed new layers of bark to embrace them and bind them all together at the base. Thus, the original trunk now emerged from a rather gruesome-looking swelling several times as wide, for it now accommodated all seven trunks, plus two more which had broken off in infancy and were going nowhere.

I was unsure where I was going next with this contemplative reconstruction of an oak tree, but my concentration was broken by the realisation that a neighbouring oak a little to my left had mysteriously grafted a red squirrel onto its trunk about five feet off the ground, and that it was staring at me from a limbs-akimbo posture with its tail facing straight up the tree, and its head facing down. It looked for all the world as if the owner of the hobbit-hole had had it skinned and mounted as a hunting trophy, except that if memory serves, hobbits are good guys and above such things. Perhaps the squirrel read my mind, for even as the notion settled there, it raced to the ground, cleared the burn in a single bound and vanished among the tall edges of the nearest spruces.

When I finally stepped out of the hobbit-hole it was to find the over-world in a state of transformation. The wind had faded away, the frost had all but vanished, the sun had emerged pallid and bleary-eyed, and the mountains across the loch had begun to materialise as the clouds rose and frayed and whitened and yellowed. My mood rose too with the mood of the day, with the mood of nature. I have been asked more than once whether I know any tricks of the trade to counter nature in its most introverted moods, ruses to lighten the burden of the gloomy days. I don't. My way is to become nature myself to the best of my ability, to become landscape myself, to blend in, to immerse, whatever the mood of the hour. When nature comes across as dark and introverted, I go dark and introverted myself. And the converse is also true. I don't flick switches to meet nature's changing moods, it simply happens with no obvious effort on my part. My purpose in nature's company is to write it down, all of it, all of its colours and colourlessness, all of its states of mind and of mindlessness. It seems to me that I am at my most effective from that point of view when I fit in.

Whenever I walk here in conditions clear enough to see the skyline ridges across the loch, I scan them and sweep their skies with binoculars, looking for eagles. Golden eagles nest not far away and to the east, the west and the north of the loch, and I see them regularly working that far skyline, or soaring a thousand feet above it. Several times, too, I have seen them cross the loch high up and from east to west, which suggests at the very least that the loch is not necessarily a territorial boundary. There again, in autumn and early winter, golden eagles tend to relax territorial boundaries, and occasionally families – or a family and a wandering immature bird – will team up and fly together, making unforgettable spectacle for the earthbound nature writer. Once, and only once, when I lived in Glen Dochart and there were two golden eagle territories in the hills behind my rented cottage, and another a couple of miles further north, I saw six golden eagles in the sky together. The gathering appeared to be completely amicable, the birds simply soared and circled. They were together for about half an hour, then, as if some consensus had been reached, they scattered in pairs across the sky and the thing was done. A month later, early in the New Year, birds at all three nesting territories were displaying vigorously.

The newcomers around the skylines above Loch Lubnaig are the sea eagles. They are not nesting here yet, although I am as sure as I can be that it is a question of time. But they turn up with increasing frequency, mostly wandering young birds, and some of these will be crossing the country between the relatively new sea eagle reintroduction site on the Tay estuary and the well-established golden and sea eagle populations on Mull, following a loosely defined two-way coast-to-coast highway, a phenomenon I explored in a book called *The Eagle's Way* (Saraband, 2014). Everything I have seen since then reinforces my conviction that not only is the "highway" in regular use in both directions, and involving the young of both species of eagles, but I am also convinced now that this is the resumption of very old behaviour, made possible once again because the east coast reintroduction of sea eagles recreated the circumstances which facilitated it. Here in the hills surrounding the loch, their vast silhouettes grace my sky, mostly alone, sometimes companionably travelling with young golden eagles, sometimes being aggressively moved on by nesting golden eagles.

Even at this distance, you can tell the eagle species apart. The sea eagle with its wings held wide has the look more of a vulture than an eagle. It is also the only thing in our sky that makes a golden eagle look small. I have seen a male golden eagle and a female sea eagle square up to each other, and although David and Goliath comparisons are uncalled for, the golden eagle looked positively compact, the sea eagle something of an ungainly monstrosity. Surprising as it may have looked at first glance, the odds were stacked against the sea eagle from the outset. Firstly, the golden eagle had the added impetus of defending its territory and there is no greater stimulus in nature. Secondly, the golden eagle is the finest flier in the sky. The sea eagle was out-thought and out-manoeuvred, and several times during a confrontation which lasted for three or four minutes it had clearly no idea where the golden eagle was, and where its next assault was coming from.

Yet where they live and breed close together and in significant numbers, as on Mull and Skye for example, they appear to function as complementary tribes, for the sea eagle is well accustomed to frequent and to hunt the low-lying ground where people live and work, while the golden eagle mostly shuns humanity and its works. I think we are not too far away from the time when the sea eagle will be restored to much of its historic landscape, and for sure the hills around Loch Lubnaig will come to know it well.

I wandered back down the lochside, thinking not about eagles (for a long scrutiny of the skyline had revealed none) but rather how that thick early frost had scarcely made it through the morning before this most un-winter-like winter dismissed it. By the time I was back at my car, I was carrying my winter jacket, for I had dressed for a cold day, and by any

standards of a Scottish winter solstice, the temperature had
risen to something uncomfortably warm.

◉ ◉ ◉

A bustling thrust of the jetstream introduced the day of the
midwinter solstice at 3a.m. with a shuddering gale and thudding rain. Seven hours later, ill-slept, I walked out near Stirling Castle. Without doubt, it was snowing in the mountains,
but the weather forecast was as fragmentary and chaotic as
ever. A burst of low sunlight from somewhere behind my left
shoulder thrust a torn, jiving fragment of rainbow in among
the snow clouds. The light show was captivating while it
lasted, and tomorrow there would be an hour or two of clear
skies, and the mountains would soar in wintry splendour, and
then it would rain and rain and the snow would vanish, the
rivers swell and churn, the fields below the foothills would
gather large and small pools of floodwater, and the geese
and the swans would flock there because there is nothing
they like better than feeding on grass through shallow water.
For now, there was the rainbow again, and again and again,
for it flashed on and off over half an hour like a landlocked
lighthouse with ideas above its station and a tendency to
jazzy improvisation.

Something eerily similar drifted through the following
afternoon when I was walking up in the Sma' Glen, not far
from Aberfeldy in Perthshire. The sun materialised in the late
afternoon this time, and it was as low and pale and round and
watchable as a full moon, and draped in hanging silken veils
of translucent snow cloud, which shifted restlessly against the

light. It was the flimsiest, frailest phenomenon I have ever seen in a Highland sky. These clouds had been at work in the glen all day, edged along from time to time by a light and chilled northerly air. Eventually the sun held sway over them for a midday hour so that the newly whitened mountains bared their shoulders and then their summits, and these shone a fetching shade of bridal white. But then the veils regathered, and layer on layer they dimmed and shaded and shackled the sun. As the afternoon edged towards the earliest of dusks, the sun appeared to recede further and further back among the fusing densities of more and more layers of cloud with their freighting of light snow, until at last it was nothing but the light at the end of a cloud tunnel, illuminating nothing at all.

NATURE WRITER

Clouds in a river pool,
yesterday's snow on the bank,
the fall of an otter's paw
memorialised there
at least until the thaw.

Every reflected river hue
- dull green, off-white, off-black,
patched sky-blue snared
between upended trees – all these
gather in the drake goosander's breast.

Raven, high and flying west,
staccato whoops slung at intervals
between the milestones
of its purpose.

SOLSTICE

And who's this whose
masking stillness slips only
to reach for that cup
of cooling flask tea
on its saucer of snow,
or to inch the pencil
that pauses at intervals
slung between the milestones
of his purpose?

Chapter Eight

Wolf Moon

SOMETIMES, WHEN I HAVE wolves on my mind, I go to Beinn
a' Chrulaiste. By the standards of its nearest neighbours it
is an unprepossessing mountain (it lives across the Glencoe
road from Meall a' Bhùiridh and Buachaille Etive Mòr,
and it rubs shoulders with the Aonach Eagach on one side
and Rannoch Moor on the other). It even has an unprepossessing name – *crulaist* means "rocky hill", so Beinn a'
Chrulaiste means "rocky hill mountain". The old namers of
that landscape that fringes Rannoch Moor didn't burn the
midnight oil of their creative imagination to come up with
that one, did they? There again, perhaps there was a time
when the mountain was just called An Crulaist because it
had a particularly rocky profile when viewed from where
the namers lived, then some academic twat with a degree in
pedantry went on a Highland jaunt, paused a night in the
Kings House Hotel, and decided to affix the prefix which
was already built into the name; and once it was written
down on a map, no one could be bothered to change it back,
for the local folk didn't need the map and went on calling
it An Crulaist, and the mountaineers who did need the map
called it what it said on the map without much caring what

it meant. But despite its name, Beinn a' Chrulaiste has rare qualities. I am predisposed to any mountain that assists the idea of an imaginative understanding of how the landscape works, and for that matter, the idea of wolf reintroduction into Highland Scotland, which is why, sometimes, when I have wolves on my mind, I go to Beinn a' Chrulaiste.

Mostly, when I do have wolves on my mind, it is midwinter. Winter is the wolf time. In countries where they still run free and where they are still permitted to make the rules which govern all nature there, winter is the season when wolves are at their most imperious. When all their prey species are weakened by winter, and especially the deer, wolves grow stronger. It can never get too cold for wolves; they are too well designed, too well insulated. On firm, dry ground, a healthy deer will always outrun a wolf, but in snow the deer struggle and the wolves are tireless. Snowy winters are when wolves effect decisive measures to adjust the balance between the deer herds and the well-being of the land. So they are not simply supreme hunters, they are also eco-warriors. One of the comparatively few human beings on Earth to grasp the true significance of that was an American ecologist, Paul L. Errington. In a book called *Of Predation and Life* (Iowa State University Press, 1967), published five years after his death, he wrote:

> *In my opinion, native predators belong in our natural outdoor scenes, not so much because they have a monetary value ... as because they are a manifestation of life's wholeness ... Predation is part of the equation of life.*

Errington also wrote:

Of all the native biological constituents of a northern wilder-
ness scene, I should say that the wolves present the greatest test
of human wisdom and good intentions.

He was an enlightened thinker on the subject of wilderness,
but then he had studied at the University of Wisconsin with
none other than Aldo Leopold, who became his mentor
and friend, and with whom he enjoyed a close working
relationship. And Leopold had numbered John Muir among
his friends, so there would have been conversations in the
University of Wisconsin at which I would love to have been
a fly on the wall.

And it was Leopold who wrote in *A Sand County Almanac*:

... I have lived to see state after state extirpate its wolves. I
have watched the face of many a newly wolfless mountain, and
seen the south-facing slopes wrinkle with a maze of new deer
trails. I have seen every edible bush and seedling browsed, first
to anaemic desuetude, and then to death ... Such a moun-
tain looks as if someone had given God pruning shears, and
forbidden Him all other exercise ... I now suspect that just as a
deer herd lives in mortal fear of its wolves, so does a mountain
live in mortal fear of its deer ...

In a Scottish context, this kind of thinking does not go down
well, even today, with the manipulators of those two great
oxymorons of our landscape, the deer forest and the grouse
moor. The idea that "predators are a manifestation of life's

wholeness" is not one that would sit lightly on the shoulders of most Highland estate land managers, far less that "predation is part of the equation of life". Unless of course the predation is done by human beings with shotguns who are paying dearly for the privilege, and who have no feeling for where they are and no sense of responsibility for the well-being of land and landscape, nor of nature and deer, nor of the native people; and to whom the idea of deferring to the wolf as top predator is an abhorrence. The economics of sporting estates are an affront to the land itself and to the deer. I love red deer, love to watch them thunder over a bealach from a high mountain perch, love to find them placidly browsing a sunlit woodland corner (they are woodland beasts at heart), love to come close and listen to their conversations. But I despise what passes for Scottish land use policy has done to them. We have been accustomed for far too long to the reckless proliferation of deer, to pruning-sheared mountains and to the absence of wolves. We have lost the capacity, the inclination and the willingness to consult our mountains, to listen to our land.

Beinn a' Chrulaiste is unquestionably a mountain that lives in mortal fear of its deer, a mountain that makes its own eloquent case for the return of the wolf. The first time I climbed it was also the moment I began to piece together the case for reintroducing wolves into a majestic Scottish Highland heartland with Rannoch Moor as its centrepiece. I was attracted to Beinn a' Chrulaiste first because of its heroic stance in the north-west corner of the Moor, and diagonally opposed to another heroic mountain in the south-east corner – Schiehallion. The first time I advanced the argument in print was twenty years now, in a book called *Gulfs of Blue Air* (Mainstream, 1997). That book was my own contribution to the age-old Scottish literary tradition of the Highland Journey. It included a crossing of Rannoch Moor:

I had crossed the Moor once before, at the end of an old March, when it was still hard and still and steely and ice-grey and dark, dark brown. I have wandered out into it in every season from Kingshouse for a mile or two at a time, just sensing the difference. I have stared out at it from Beinn Dorain, Schiehallion, and the Buachaille's near neighbour, Beinn a' Chrulaiste, the last an occasion when it contrived its own sunrise weather, fashioned it into a thunderous storm and hurled that monster of its own making at mighty Clach Lethad of the Black Mount, resuming (as I saw it, high and dry on my off-to-one-side mountain) ancient glacial hostilities. If you ever fall to wondering about the ice-bound forces which made the shape of the Highlands as we know them, then scratch your head over this: Rannoch Moor was once a high white plateau, like the Icelandic ice cap or northern Greenland. When things began to move, and the dragging weight of the ice began to fashion mountains, Rannoch Moor fell through its own roof and lay there, a reservoir of ice, and the glaciers of the embryonic Black Mount fed off it. I have stood on an Icelandic glacier (it is no great claim to fame, any number of tourists have done it), and although any number of films and glossy books can prepare you for the spectacle if not the scale of the spectacle, nothing had prepared me for the fact that it spoke. It groaned and growled and muttered and spat out lumps of itself. It sounded like the indecipherable musings of a parliament of plotting architects:

should we have another lake here, another mountain? Or a mountain range? If we lay our moraines through that valley, will trees follow? It was a millionth part – a billionth for all I know – of an awareness of what went on here when Rannoch Moor invented itself and began to leak glaciers of its own – Glen Orchy, Glen Etive, Glencoe, and east to Loch Rannoch, even northwards where Loch Ericht lies. My mind is not up to the task of imagining what that re-invention of landscapes must have looked like, but I have heard a few syllables of the language of the architects.

Over the years I refined and elaborated on my wolf reintroduction argument, in *Brother Nature* (Whittles, 2003), most noticeably in *The Last Wolf* (Birlinn, 2010), and most recently in my beaver book, *Nature's Architect* (Saraband, 2015). The plan is this: a new wilderness national park extending from the Black Wood of Rannoch and Rannoch Moor to the Black Mount, Glen Orchy and Inishail, and west to the shore of Loch Etive. The national park should mean what it says – a park owned by the nation, rather than the unwieldy conglomerations of often reluctant landowners that characterise Scotland's existing national parks. Its overwhelming priorities would be to serve the needs of nature. Its every native habitat would be enhanced, extended, restored; Rannoch Moor would return to the lightly wooded mosaic it once was. The first wolf reintroduction would be into the Black Wood and the Moor of Rannoch, and because the new national park would march with the Cairngorms National Park in the north-east and Loch Lomond and the Trossachs National Park to the south-west, the wolves would be well served with room to expand in both directions. I think that initially at least, Scotland could accommodate three or four packs, and if numbers increased beyond that, some controlling measures could be considered. It is a model that seems to work well in Norway, where wolves re-introduced themselves by walking over the border from Sweden. In the absence of a land border with Sweden or anywhere else for that matter, we, the people, have to make the first move. We have nothing to fear. On the contrary, when the wolf's wholly benevolent presence is revealed to us, an ancient darkness locked deep within our psyche will be banished. For the wolf is a catalyst, an enabler, a provider of unlimited opportunity for nature in all its guises, all its tribes. Like aconites and snowdrops thrusting through frozen ground to burst into flower, wolves invigorate the land with new light, new colour, a new flowering.

All the obstacles are in our minds. We misunderstand the nature of the wolf. That ancient darkness from which the old stories emanated and elaborated their distortions (a devourer of babies, a despoiler of the battlefield dead) is the product of nothing more than a very old storytelling tradition. The real wild wolf is to be found elsewhere. And despite all that biologists now know about the wolf in many countries, despite all the literature and all the television documentaries, despite the Yellowstone reintroduction making positive headlines for wolves around the world, there are still far too many of us who believe, or think we believe, that the only good wolf is a dead wolf, or better still, an extinct wolf.

Even the myths are stubborn. There was a strange story in some British newspapers on January 12th, 2017, concerning the full moon that night. It said that the first full moon of the year is known as the wolf moon. I had never heard of a wolf moon, so with years of dismantling wolf myths under my belt I was immediately suspicious. The story explained that it was so named because in the deep snow of midwinter, wolf packs got hungry and came in around the villages of Native American tribes, scavenging for food. The implication, at least, was that the food walked around on two legs.

So far, so much bollocks. But why, I wondered, would British newspapers run such a story? Where had it come from? I sniffed around. I have a background of newspaper journalism, and although I quit my last staff job almost thirty years ago to write my books, sometimes it still serves me well. It turned out that the 2017 edition of an American journal called the *Farmers' Almanac* was its 200th, and so it had issued press releases and posted blogs in celebration. And because one of the ingredients was the wolf – and I can see no other explanation – it found its way into some very unlikely outlets, which you could be forgiven for thinking are normally furth of the fiefdom of the *Farmers' Almanac*. It said that native tribes among America's northern and eastern states used to name each full moon (which is true), and the first of the year was the wolf moon (which, it turned out, isn't). The *Almanac* elaborated on the reason why the first moon of the year was called the wolf moon:

Amid the cold and deep snows of midwinter, the wolf packs howled hungrily outside Indian villages.

Oh did they, indeed? There are two problems here. The first is that wolves don't "howl hungrily". They howl to talk to each other over distance. And they do it at different times of the day and night and at all phases of the moon and when there is no moon at all. They do it when they're hungry, they do it when their bellies are full, they do it to announce their presence, their numbers, their state of health, their territorial boundaries. Howling is wolf-to-wolf conversation and it is pack-bonding. It has nothing to do with snow or hunger or January. Or the moon.

The second problem is that wolves don't go hungry "amid the cold and deep snows of winter" because as I have already explained, (a) it can never get too cold for wolves, and (b) deep snow is when wolves are at their strongest and their prey at its weakest. They feed sumptuously in midwinter, and the surplus from the unfinished kills they leave behind feeds many, many other mouths. They had no need whatever to go anywhere near a village in the north-eastern states in winter, and they know from a few thousand years of their history that there are very sound reasons for avoiding human settlements, the most pressing of which is that they get shot.

Even if there were tribes that referred to the first full moon of the year as the wolf moon, then that still doesn't explain the story. I went in search of those conspicuously unnamed tribes, and you will be less than amazed to discover that I found none. What I did find was a Native American Studies source that listed all the names of all the moons (for they are all named, in much the same way as we name the months). Then I narrowed the list down to the tribes of the northern and north-eastern states, and this is what I found for January, the first full moon of the year:

Abenaki – greetings maker moon; Algonquin – sun has

no strength to thaw moon; Anishinaabe – great spirits moon; Cherokee – cold moon; Cree – moon when the old fellow spreads the brush; Lakota – hard moon; Mohawk – the big cold moon; Passamaquoddy – whirling wind moon; Potawatomi – moon of the bear; Winnebago – fish running moon; and Sioux – wolves run together moon, the only wolf reference. There was no other mention of a specific wolf moon for any tribe anywhere; this despite the fact that there were moons named for eagle, grey goose, snow goose, frog, ducks moult, and birds fly south.

I could be uncharitable and say that this was the farmers using their magazine to spread a little seasonal anti-wolf propaganda, but even if that were the case, it does not excuse newspapers in this country publishing such rot. But our 21st-century media, as in many other northern hemisphere countries, cannot resist taking a potshot at wolves. In general, basic journalistic principles – like a respect for truth and thorough research – are abandoned when the subject is nature, and when it is the wolf then the level of abandonment goes into overdrive. Exaggeration, misinformation, jokes and profound ignorance characterise the coverage. It has been that way for a long time. But there is no longer an excuse. It took me about fifteen minutes to pull the story apart. When I wrote *The Last Wolf*, it took me a day and a half to prove to my entire satisfaction that the story of the death of Scotland's last wolf up the River Findhorn in 1743 was a work of pure fiction. Yet it has been unquestioningly regurgitated since 1829 (when it was first written down) and still reappears even in some nature conservation thinking uttered by people who should really know better.

This is what the wolf is up against.

This is what champions of wolf reintroduction are up against, and ahead lies a lengthy struggle to overwhelm the forces of ignorance, indifference and downright hostility from much of Scotland's landowning class.

But my best guess is that the wolves will be back. The climate has begun to inch away from the dark forces of Victorian prejudice to which much of Scottish land management practice still clings. Community buy-outs of estates have forced their way on to the political and social agenda of the land. In December 2016, the Arkaig Community Trust, in partnership with Woodland Trust Scotland, announced the purchase of 2,500 acres of Scots pine woodland above Loch Arkaig in Inverness-shire, having raised £500,000 in nine months. The woodland was described as "degraded", but the management strategy is based on the restoration and expansion of a key native habitat. The move is symptomatic of a new optimism that has begun to enliven social and political debate in Scotland, at the heart of which is a new relationship with the land, with nature.

And just a month earlier, the Scottish Government approved the formal reintroduction of beavers into Scotland after a five-year official trial in Argyll and the simultaneous emergence of a slightly less official population on Tayside accumulated from mysterious sources, but demonstrably thriving. The government courageously announced that its decision would embrace both groups, despite sustained hostility from farmers in Angus and Perthshire which included random shooting of beavers and setting snares on dams and lodges. Both beaver groups would be allowed to expand their range naturally, and other areas of Scotland would be targeted for reintroductions.

The precedent is a significant one for wolves. Reintroduction of bird species had always been regarded as a more straightforward process, but a significant mammal with a capacity to redesign its chosen landscape, creating and expanding wetland, slowing the flow of watercourses, making new habitats and opportunities for a vast range of species of fish, plants, insects and birds … all that indicates a willingness in government and nature conservation to challenge the old order, to make a space for new thinking. All that must mean that there is a greater likelihood now than at any time in the last 200 years for the return of the wolf to Scotland.

It was in that frame of mind that three days after the last snowfall of the winter (so far advanced was March that it was also just one day before the clocks went forward), I headed back to the Rannoch-Moor-facing flank of Beinn a' Chrulaiste. As was the way throughout that winter, no sooner had the snow fallen than the temperature climbed again, and what I found was a land in transition again. There was sunlight, but there was also a high, thin damask of cloud. The mountains were zebra-striped with snow and dark rock. The Moor wore all the wolf shades from dark brown through all the shades of grey and the slate of pools and lochans, all of it shot through with the white of old snow patches, a confetti of white. It occurred to me that twenty wolves could walk across that spreadeagled land and I would be lucky to see one of them.

I mention this because Beinn a' Chrulaiste is a mountain which lives in mortal fear of its deer, and because wolves and deer and Rannoch Moor were part of my purpose on the mountain. And because of the red deer hinds clustered within yards of the car park of the Kings House right under Beinn a' Chrulaiste when I parked there. Such an occurrence is by no means unusual in Highland Scotland, which has been wolfless for more than 200 years now, and in that time the deer have forgotten how to behave like deer. Studies at Yellowstone have shown how deer quickly re-learn forgotten behaviour in the company of reintroduced wolves. The very presence of wolves keeps the deer herds on the move so that the impact on the land of their relentless grazing is reduced immediately. I asked Beinn a' Chrulaiste what it thought of the idea of a wilderness national park with wolves right here, and it agreed with me.

For nineteen consecutive weeks through the summer and early autumn of 2001, I paused under Beinn a' Chrulaiste at midnight. I had been asked to give a talk every Tuesday evening to a different group of American visitors on board a small cruise ship that was moored for the night at Neptune's Staircase, a majestic chain of locks on the Caledonian Canal. It was a delightful commission. The audiences were warm and engaged, the meal I shared with them was excellent, the job paid well, and the drive between Glen Dochart (where I lived at the time) and the ship's berth a little to the west of Fort William was hardly a hardship. Every week, more or less around midnight, my drive home wound up through the tight black-rock curves of the Pass of Glencoe, and then the road would open out to accommodate the broad miles of Rannoch Moor on my left, the mountains of the Black Mount on my right. Immediately before that there was the small matter of passing between the scene-stealer (Buachaille Etive Mòr) and the unsung off-to-one-side mountain, Beinn a' Chrulaiste. And every week, I crept along that long, straight road among hundreds and hundreds of red deer. Just past Beinn a' Chrulaiste, I slipped into a layby, wound down the window, switched off the engine and tuned in to the midnight secrecies of the red deer.

As far as I could see, there were two reasons for the gathering. One was that the lush grass on the roadside verge was off-limits during the daytime because of the volume of traffic. After midnight, mine was often the only car on the road for miles at a time.

The second reason was that they liked the warmth of the road and lay down on it. Sometimes I had to treat them like roundabouts. Here was the living proof of Aldo Leopold's theory. Here were fearless deer in a wolfless landscape, deer which had long since forgotten how to behave like their ancestors behaved when they shared the land with wolves. And there was the mountain that lived in mortal fear of so many deer. If you climb Beinn a' Chrulaiste by the burn that feeds into the River Etive near the Kings House, you can count the number of trees on the mountain as you climb. One.

Such is the legacy of the wolfless years, the God-with-the-pruning-shears years. The memory drifted back into mind when I pulled in to the Kings House on a late March day of 2017, and I found a posse of red deer dozing by the car park.

I sought out the company of the burn which emerges into the overworld from the unknowable inner heart of the mountain among its summit rocks. The re-interpretation of that burn as a kind of pulmonary artery of the mountain is irresistible, ferrying lifeblood to the landscape's lungs, sustenance for all nature, and nature writers for that matter. Just below the watershed I sat in pale sunlight on a rock in the middle of the burn and between two talkative little waterfalls, a notebook and a map in my lap, a sandwich in my hand and the makings of a cup of tea. I fished the teabag from the cup with a finger and in the process I spilled tea over a few square inches of the Ordnance Survey's idea of Rannoch Moor. I immediately thought of Sweet Medwin Water, of *that* map, *those* stains. I wiped the Rannoch tea, watched the residue darken, and left it where it was. The tradition is alive and well, George, on this off-to-one-side mountain between Glencoe and Rannoch, as it was in the southern Pentland Hills. The rock where I sat was pale pink, and the melting snow had imbued the burn with a hint of the green of glaciers in its pools and glimmers of yellow in its cataracts and small falls.

For an hour, possibly longer, I did nothing at all but look around, drinking tea and burn water, and drinking in that astounding land. Slowly I realised that the peculiarities of the light and that high, thin cloud conferred on the snow the frailest, the palest, the iciest shade of blue you ever saw. Yet that very frailty of that blue was all-pervasive, for it was held fast and underpinned in every large and small fragment of snow. And every snow fragment was in turn buttressed and secured by black rock and dark brown heather stems, but then again these seemed to be held in place by the snow. But the blue was as transient as eggshells and the whole effect was of a phenomenon that might crack apart in a million places at once and the whole palette of the landscape collapse, or slide away into gullies, burns, rivers.

The temperature climbed into the early afternoon, the wind drifted away, and I could almost sense the mountain shaking itself free of the warming, dwindling snow – like a wolf. On my way down, the change in the underfoot conditions was marked. The whole hillside was charged with the movement of impromptu burns and waterslides, so many of them that I was struck with an image of migrating eels, albeit it a downstream migration. They burbled and gurgled. They mumbled, rumbled and tumbled. They wriggled, giggled and jiggled. They croaked and joked. They glittered and chattered. They tripped and skipped. And the Allt a' Ballaich, the mountain pulmonary, drank them all and surged on its way down to the distant glen of the River Etive.

Back at the car park, a tourist minibus had decanted its passengers beside the deer, some of which had walked right up to the bus, clearly in expectation of being hand-fed. I have no doubt the visitors get a kick out of the encounter. God knows what the deer get out of it, but none of it will be healthy.

Once the bus had gone, they went back to browsing and drowsing. One grey-faced old hind lay in a flat-out curve on the grass. She hadn't moved to greet the bus. When she lay with her chin in the moss and her ears erect (and with the notable absence of a thick tail to wrap round her muzzle), there was a moment when I thought she looked like nothing so much as an old wolf.

If you drive south between the edge of Rannoch Moor and the mountains of the Black Mount, as I did in the late afternoon of the last day of winter, you should pause to have a look out at the Moor just where there is a cluster of lochans not far from the road. The islands in the lochans reveal the true nature of this land, which is that it should be lightly wooded. They reveal it only because no deer graze there. Any crossing of the Moor reveals the same thing, except that the only evidence of trees you encounter is their broken, long-dead bones protruding from the peat. Too many deer impoverish the land, and then because the land is impoverished and cannot sustain so many deer, the health of the deer herds themselves is also impoverished.

Remember Paul Errington, writing in 1967:

> *Of all the native biological constituents of a northern wilderness scene, I should say that the wolves present the greatest test of human wisdom and good intentions.*

Watching the old hind with the wolf face I thought that, fifty years later, it's time to put our wisdom and good intentions to the test. It's long past time.

Chapter Nine

Hark the Herald Eagle

Mountain dark at the year's end
then hark! the herald eagle
(a golden ray):
"I am the Light."

THE PLANET WE INHABIT spins on its axis in deepest midwinter
in such a way that it begins to draw closer to the sun, even
as we tend to draw closer towards the fire. But regardless
of what the thermometer may tell us, regardless of what
winter may yet have to throw at us, an irrevocable process
of warming and brightening is already dimly underway. The
darkest days and the longest nights are already behind us,
and nothing in nature misses the change, unless of course it's
hibernating. You could be forgiven for thinking that the first
place to mark the change would be somewhere mild in the
west, perhaps a shoreline lulled by the Gulf Stream where
palm trees nod agreeably in gardens. But it is not so. The first
truly conspicuous indication that winter is on the wane is
one of grand gestures, and high in the landlocked mountains
at that, and even while winter still seethes.

At the rounded end of a dipping hill shoulder, I was

pretending to be a small piece of the big rock at my back. It is at a little over 1,500 feet, and somewhere in that wild and roadless terrain between the glens of Balquhidder and Dochart. The rock is on more or less level ground, the first respite after the steep plod up from one of those small cul-de-sac glens that plough deep into the hills then abruptly seem to think better of the idea. The shoulder climbs away from the rock, rises in a series of false summits to a rough cairn a thousand feet higher.

I sat there because quarter of an hour ago now I saw a golden eagle climbing in wide spirals up through one of those vast internal spaces enclosed by the flanks of the big hills. Then as it reached some kind of zenith in its own mind, it drifted south on the north wind towards the summit of this very hill. As it happens, I know this eagle, or at least I recognise it: a male, almost universally dark, a kind of mahogany shade, except that those feathers on the nape of his neck that ornithology decided long ago were of a distinctive enough shade to christen the bird "golden"…that feathered headdress seemed to me to have a particular burnish. I know where it is accustomed to nest. I also have a rough idea (very rough – I have no grasp at all of how a golden eagle thinks) of how it defines its territory. After years spent watching the same two pairs on adjacent territories, I have begun to believe that the boundaries may be determined not by distance or geographical features but rather by flying time away from the nest, and so the boundaries of territory will fluctuate with the wind direction. But when golden eagles mark out their territories, when they begin to restate their claim, when they embark upon their own idea of the annual festival of New

Year, they do so by display-flying above the same promi-
nent landscape features. However flexible the boundaries of
territory may be on a day-to-day basis, year after year they
announce their renewed presence to the rest of the watching
world in the same places, and these may (I'm guessing again)
mark the territory's non-negotiable core.

So I sat with the big rock at my back because I saw the
eagle climb and drift towards the summit of the long hill
shoulder, and because I know from many hours spent here
over many old winters, that this particular hill shoulder is
important in that particular eagle's scheme of things. And as
I sat, I told myself this: if the eagle in question is about to do
what I think it may be about to do, then I am in the right
place at the right time, and this could be good. I faced south,
the rock shielding me from the north wind, and I prepared
for the near certainty of getting very cold very slowly.

An hour later I *was* very cold, but still, I reassured myself,
I *was* in the right place, and the right time would be along
any minute now …

Another hour, still facing south, still scanning the sky, and
trying to suppress the memory from one old spring not far
from this rock of sitting watching a perched golden eagle do
nothing at all for four hours. And then suddenly he appeared
far in the south, very high and very small. I had found him
by chance with a slow sweep of my binoculars across the sky,
perhaps the 20th such slow sweep. And yet, it wasn't chance
that led me here, it wasn't chance that commanded me to
sit, it wasn't chance that imposed stillness and patience on
the sitting and the waiting, and it wasn't chance that finally
fulfilled my expectation of seeing him there, sooner or later. I

write about what happens, of course, not about the hundreds of blank hours over thirty-something years when nothing at all happens except the slow seepage of awareness, experience, and acceptance between the mountain and the watcher.

"This way," I muttered aloud to no one at all, "this way."

I saw the eagle tilt, change direction, and vanish going *that* way, checked my watch, decided on a time limit. One more hour sitting still on this hill shoulder in this hazy grey weather and its persistent north wind would be quite enough. I don't know why I do that, because events inevitably determine the timespan of the vigil. Almost certainly, I will not notice the moment when fifty-nine minutes tick over to sixty. The passage of time will have nothing to do with it. I look at my watch when there is nothing going on. When things are happening, who knows where the time goes?

So the trick then is to find a way to renew the commitment to the watching. You have to intensify the scrutiny. An old eagle man I used to know once told me that when you are looking for golden eagles "you must learn to scan the middle distance". It's a tall order sometimes, and it is never as easy as it sounds, not least because there is often nothing in your middle distance to focus on. You must explore the three-dimensional space between you and the next piece of land. But you get the hang of it with practice. So I set about devouring the middle distance of the space between me and the limit of what I suspect might be the eagle's territory, and I tried it with and without the binoculars … the narrow view and the wide view. If I was right, if I was still in the right place, one more cold hour (or whatever it took) would be a small price to pay.

A hint of brightness stole over the sky in the south-west. A single stag came and stood on a corner of a skyline buttress. I watched it for a while with binoculars and then without, putting it into the context of its colossal landscape. Then I rebuked myself, for I was watching a fixed point of land, not scrutinising the middle distance. Settle again, readjust everything that can be readjusted – the mat I was sitting on, the position of my back against the rock, the zip of my jacket, the cuffs of the jacket so that they embrace my gloves more snugly, my state of mind (become landscape rather than a man in a jacket with binoculars; stop fussing with the binoculars; be still, or at least as still as humanly possible – if you must move, make small movements and make them slowly).

The middle distance became the centre of the world. There came a point in the passage of time when I started to see that space as a thing of its own, with colours of its own, a three-dimensional object as tangible as a mountain. Somewhere deep inside myself I smiled. Better.

A new wind came, curving round the rock at my back, exploring my right cheek, a light gust that danced on almost at once, but leaving its mark on my cheek for a while. I heard a crow, then a raven, then both together. I sought them both out because of that ancient symbiosis by which golden eagle and mountain corvids are forever bound, and which has offered countless scraps of encouragement over several decades to this watcher of eagles. But these two appeared to be shouting at each other, the crow perched, the raven adrift close to the stag's buttress. Either that or I was missing something. It occurred to me then as my binoculars briefly followed the raven that the stag had gone and I had not seen it go, because it had not been part of the middle distance.

Then there was a sudden movement, a movement so sudden that its very suddenness startled me. It was a movement not of a golden eagle but of my own head, turning to the right. Suddenly.

Why turn at that moment?

There had been no sound, nothing lodged in the corner of my eye, not even that playful wind. Instead, there was … a shift, a waft of awareness, a stirring of that other indefinable sense that grafts itself onto you over the years like lichen on an Ardgour oak tree, so imperceptibly that you were unaware of its presence until suddenly you put it to use.

And there was the eagle.

Falling.

Falling as nothing on Earth falls, and nothing in Earth's sky.

Falling as a state of grace.

Falling as an art form, with beauty and purpose.

The shape of a falling golden eagle is an abstraction, almost a diamond, but a diamond tampered with by nature's take on the science of aerodynamics, and squared off at the top and curved to a point at the base. In its falling, the eagle looked as dark as mahogany, except that the new brightness that had begun to infuse the sky also infused the nape of the eagle, that mercurially light-sensitive hood of feathers, that "golden". In different lights it can catch your eye as anything between tawny and auburn, and in almost no light at all it transforms again: an extraordinary photograph by my friend Laurie Campbell, and published in my book, *The Eagle's Way*, shows a golden eagle on the island of Harris asleep on a ledge near its eyrie at midsummer midnight, and that same mercurial hood is somewhere between ash grey and white. But on this falling eagle excavating an eagle-shaped shaft through the middle distance of mountain air somewhere above Balquhidder Glen in the Loch Lomond and the Trossachs National Park, that new light in the sky glanced upon the nape in such a way that it shone, it truly shone. The same light smote the base of the eagle's bill with a vivid note of a deep daffodil yellow. Mahogany, pale gold and deep yellow ... but of course the thing was happening at a barely credible airspeed, so that from the moment it came into sight, high and to my right, until the moment it pulled out perhaps twenty feet above the hill shoulder where I sat, and well over to my left, no more than five seconds could have passed. Five seconds, but somewhere in their midst, that falling eagle breenged through the precise moment at the precise angle that cause the nape of its neck to flare with a pale gold sheen, and for what may have been no more than a second, no diamond ever shone with a finer lustre than that one.

Then it was ascending again in spirals, scratching its name on the blue-grey void of the northern sky, then it was holding up against the wind at the top of its climb, then it fell again but this time the flight took the form of a roller-coastering parade the whole length of the hill shoulder, a sequence of short wing-folded dives and towering climbs, and all of it in and out of sunlight, and all of it spilling air with brutal power and sustained elegance in perfectly equal measure. At such a moment, my sense of the world shrinks and my state of mind is one of helplessness, helpless admiration, helpless thraldom in nature's cause, helpless anguish that there are out there and not more than a couple of watersheds distant, examples of my own species who would rather poison such a bird than sit and watch it in silent wonder. It is a lot to take on, one cold afternoon of late January.

Amid the more or less limitless glories of natural flight, there are two examples of the art which astound me beyond rational thought so that they become the preserve not just of the mind but also of the heart. Both of them are at their most luminous in midwinter. One of them is this golden eagle festival by which it celebrates its own idea of a New Year, the beginning of one more long haul to establish one more new generation of its tribe; the symbolism is as irresistible as the performance to any nature writer worth the name. The other could scarcely be more different, either in the execution or in the purpose, but both have in common that they deal in grand gestures and that they are events of extraordinary power and beauty and grace. The eagle flies to proclaim its place on the map of the world, its spectacle is solitary and silent. The whooper swan is a thousand miles from home, it moves from one wintering ground to another in low and level skeins, a restless, nomadic procession from the Northern Isles or the Western Isles to Slimbridge or the Fens and back again, then when it is satisfied that winter is done, back up the northern ocean to Iceland. The conversation of these flights is a constant exchange of snatches of muted brass. The glory of them is in low sunlight, which January and February assist, so that the white plumage of their wings takes on a variety of shades from blue to orange, depending on the strength of the light and the nature of the terrain where it is flying, for there is nothing like swan plumage to absorb the shade of its surroundings. A skein of whooper swans flying into a sunset is a constant rhythmic progress of flashing lights: overwings and underwings rise and fall and respond in a four-in-the-bar jazzy way to the impact of the light source.

With the eagle gone from my sky, these were the thoughts that rummaged around in the vacuum it left behind. Eagle and swan rarely coincide, and when they do, at least in a Scottish context, it will usually be out in the Hebrides where golden eagles nest much lower than they do in the Highland heartland mountains, and where whooper swans both migrate and linger on favourite lochs and lochans. On the rare occasions when whooper swans venture into the mountains, it will be perhaps because prevailing weather conditions persuaded them to cross a mountain pass rather than fly round the mountain, and there is no doubt that some will follow the course of major glens on migration.

Once, and only once, I watched a solitary whooper swan battle against a real Hebridean gale and apparently try to cross the ridge of the Skye Cuillin at upwards of 2,000 feet. The incident is as inexplicable to me now as it was then, about twenty winters ago. An eagle can fly into a healthy headwind, half-fold its wings, and pick up speed. A swan in the same wind struggles to make headway and usually goes low and tries to fly under it.

I was still sitting with my back to the same rock on the same mountain shoulder, and had been setting my mind's eye to times and places where I had seen swan and eagle share the same airspace, and thinking how their different flight techniques suited their lifestyles – and how both appealed so much to my lifestyle – and all that came to mind were the south of Skye, the west coast of Mull, the great east-west trough of Loch Tay and Glen Dochart in Highland Perthshire, and the north-south funnel of Gleann Einich in the Cairngorms. And then I realised that the eagle was back.

It flew so low and slow above the ground at that moment that I wondered if it had just risen from a perch, and if so, where had it perched and how long had it been there, and had it been watching me? You see what happens when you switch off and stop scrutinising the middle distance? The next moment I had at least some circumstantial evidence to back up that hunch. At no more than about fifty feet above the shoulder, the eagle held up in the wind again, and like a preposterously inflated kestrel, it hung there, working wingtips and tail feathers, and I am as sure as I can be that the object at the far end of its gaze for a few moments was myself. This has happened to me three times before, and each time I had been very still for a long time, sitting against a rock that was deliberately chosen because I knew it was a landmark in a golden eagle territory. The feeling engendered by each occasion was one of profound respect, of being in the presence of one of nature's ambassadors, of briefly keeping the company of true, undiluted wildness. To a nature writer, these are scraps of gold dust. They are among the most precious souvenirs that persuaded me many years ago now to dismiss the idea of a climbing a mountain to pronounce it climbed, and to find a new way of my own in the mountain midst where I might meet and linger in the company of the natives.

The eagle banked away, leaned out into the void beyond the mountainside and began to climb, not in lazy spirals this time but straight up at an angle remarkably close to vertical, an ascent powered by a surge of huge wingbeats, hundreds of feet in a handful of seconds. At first, there was an audible pulse with each wingbeat, the sound diminishing as it climbed. Then from almost directly overhead, it began again. The eagle appeared to lean forward in the air so that its tail was almost directly above its head, then it folded its wings so that the tips were held close to the end of the tail, and in a mighty burst of speed it was falling again. The dive levelled out and curved upwards again without pause and in precisely the opposite of the position in which the dive had begun, the head now almost directly above the tail, the tail pointing back at the earth, at my rock, at me. This time the climb soared on and on, maybe a thousand feet, maybe 2,000, for the eagle was quite alone in that portion of the sky and any idea of its final altitude was far beyond reliable guesswork. Then it boarded the wind and raced south away from me.

So high up and far away a golden eagle began to sky-dance its way into my heart. It travelled a mile-long mountainside in a free-flowing sequence of power-climbs and free-falls, dismissing a thousand feet of air from its wings, ripping open the sky, climbing again, flipping over, diving down, the whole thing as rhythmic as waves, as seamless as winds. It reached the slope that dipped towards my rock. It was suddenly so close that I became more aware of the blurring hillside as I tried to keep the binoculars focussed on the bird, so I lowered them to watch with my eyes instead. Sometimes you see more clearly without binoculars. In this case, that simple action liberated everything. In particular, it restored the glorious perspective of the bird and its native heath, the mountains and all their intervening spaces and their overarching skies. I remembered a snatch of Gavin Maxwell's *Raven Seek Thy Brother* (Longman, 1968):

> ... *with the cold so bitter that I was conscious of my own shivering, I felt an actual buoyancy, an uplift of spirit. This was my world, the cradle of my species, shared with the wild creatures; it was the only world I wanted ...*

The eagle crossed the level ground where I sat, dipped a wing once more and fell from my sight. In the past two hours, the planet we inhabit had spun on its axis in such a way that it had drawn a little closer to the sun.

⊙ ⊙ ⊙

The winter of 2017 brought encouraging news about the state of Scotland's golden eagle population, with the publication by Scottish Natural Heritage (SNH) of the results of the 2015 national golden eagle survey, the first since 2003. It revealed an increase from 442 pairs in 2003 to 508 pairs in 2015. What intrigued me particularly was this sentence:

> *The North Highlands and the central spine of the country between the Great Glen and Stirlingshire saw the greatest increase in eagle numbers.*

The reference to Stirlingshire meant these very mountains, the heart of my working territory, and confirmed what I had been thinking and seeing over the previous three or four years, which seems to me to be when the recovery started to gather pace. I have been watching golden eagles here for about thirty-five years, and there are at least seven territories that have held breeding birds for at least some of that time. To my certain knowledge, four of the seven have been unoccupied for shorter or longer periods. But now I am seeing more birds more often on more of the territories.

All that suggests that something fundamental has changed, and whatever that may be, it is working to the golden eagles' advantage. It is tempting to think of a combination of factors as the most likely explanation: there is more food for them, there is less disturbance at some of the eyries, the land is being less intensively worked, or even that landowners and their gamekeepers have had a fit of conscience and have finally recognised that eagles have more of a right to the odd grouse or deer calf than their well-heeled, gun-totin' clients. No, I don't believe that one either.

There is, however, one other significant factor, one rapidly evolving circumstance which has begun to make an impact on many of nature's tribes in both Highland and Lowland landscapes. It began on the west coast, then on the east, and such is the way of these things, it has begun to make its presence felt in the mountainous heartlands. That SNH report had also noted that in 2015 Scotland had 106 breeding pairs of sea eagles. It also indulged in some uncharacteristic crystal-ball gazing and predicted numbers rising to 221 pairs by 2025 and then an explosive expansion to between 890 and 1,005 pairs by 2040.

If SNH's numbers are anything like accurate, this means that somewhere around 2030, the sea eagle will start to outnumber the golden eagle in Scotland, a proposition I first advance in *The Eagle's Way*. That book showed how a two-way coast-to-coast eagle highway had begun to evolve, a broad swathe of land roughly between the Tay estuary and the Isle of Mull. I wrote of all the ecological riches that are bound to flow back and forth from coast-to-coast travel and settlement, riches we can only guess at yet, in much the same way that no one anticipated the benevolent extent of wolf reintroduction into Yellowstone when that project began.

...The scale may be different, and Scotland is, alas, still some distance away from putting wolves back into Rannoch, but the principle of repairing a systematically raided ecosystem by installing new native blood at the top of the food chain is one that cannot fail. That, and the restoration and expansion of every native habitat is all the help nature needs to recreate something of an older, wilder order.

The first thing we will learn is that the golden eagle will not be impoverished if and when – almost certainly "when" – it is outnumbered by the sea eagle ...Mostly the two eagle tribes co-exist amicably enough. In occasional one-to-one skirmishes, usually a territorial dispute, I never seen and never heard of a sea eagle prevailing. The golden eagle is the supreme flier as well as the supreme predator of our skies, and that alone will be enough to guarantee the stability of Scotland's golden eagle presence. Inferior numbers will not change that.

A wise man, a grizzly bear guide on Kodiak Island, Alaska, called Scott Shelton, once told me: "The only way to get to know a creature is to live with it." We were speaking in his cabin on a tiny island in the middle of a lake on Kodiak where I had found moulted bald eagle feathers yards from his doorstep, and the subject under discussion was living with bears, wolves and eagles. He was experienced and adept at sharing the landscape with all of these. He was the one who convinced me by his own example that we learn about and understand other creatures only by living with them, not by taking the word of the loud mouths and small minds of those vested interests which would shout us down and have us believe that Scotland cannot accommodate those creatures their predecessors cleared from the land. Scotland can. The land can and the people can. We learn by living with them. We make adjustments and so do they ... In the same way, the two eagle tribes learned to live with each other many, many thousands of years ago.

All of which brings me back to what might account for this new prospering of the golden eagle population down the spine of the country. It occurs to me that it has coincided with a marked increase in the appearance of wandering young sea eagles in the breeding territories of those heartland golden eagles. At first, this happened mostly in winter, because golden eagles relax their territorial disciplines outwith the long haul of their nesting season, and a degree of tolerance of other eagles is a symptom of that. My own experience has been that now it happens at any time of the year, and that can only be explained by one of two possibilities. The first is that, as yet, these wandering sea eagles are just that, and because they are too young to harbour territorial ambitions of their own, the resident golden eagles don't see them as a threat. The other is that the sea eagles are providing something that the golden eagles can benefit from, and that is their sheer size and consequent power. They can kill larger prey, and like most top predators, they can kill beyond their needs and fill the mouths of others. The presence of a sea eagle on a golden eagle territory is also the presence of an extra hunter. It is also a comparatively cumbersome and conspicuous bird, so that when it does kill, the golden eagle, with its extraordinary speed and flight powers, is in a position to benefit from it immediately. A sea eagle can muscle a golden off a kill on the ground, but is no match for a pair of golden eagles.

There is also the consideration that sea eagles tend to nest at lower altitudes than golden eagles, so when they do move into those heartland mountains to nest – as they will, and have done historically – the nesting golden eagles have little to worry about. Rather, there is every indication that the golden eagles will do very well out of the relationship. They learn from each other by living in each other's company, you see, and they make adjustments.

Chapter Ten

Whale Watch (2): The Humpback's Back

A HUMPBACK WHALE turned up in the Firth of Forth in January 2017. The news of its arrival seared through me with a high-voltage shudder of dread.

Now why would a humpback whale of all creatures induce such a drastic and irrational reaction in a nature writer of all creatures? Especially when you consider that the humpback in particular among the great whales has endeared itself to generation after generation of writers. Henry Melville, whose Moby Dick is the most celebrated of humpbacks, and arguably the most celebrated of whales, wrote of it thus:

He is the most gamesome and light-hearted of all whales, making more gay foam and white water generally than any other of them.

Roger Payne, an American whale biologist who is also the author of my favourite whale book – *Among Whales* (Scribner, 1998) – wrote:

> *...what captivates me most about them is their songs. During their breeding season, humpback whales produce long, complex sequences of sounds that can be heard by listening through a hydrophone...These songs are much longer than bird songs and can last up to thirty minutes, though fifteen is nearer the norm. They are divided into repeating phrases called themes. When the phrase is heard to change (usually after a few minutes), it heralds the start of a new theme. Songs contain from two to nine themes and are strung together without pauses so a long singing session is an exuberant river of sound that can flow on for twenty-four hours or longer.*

And I agree with both of those writers.

And I have seen a humpback at its most gamesome and light-hearted, making enough gay foam and white water to last me a lifetime. And I have looked directly into the four-inch-wide eyeball of a humpback whale as I leaned over the gunwale of a small whale-watching boat in Glacier Bay, Alaska, and the whale slid past less than six feet below me and a yard out from the boat, and I felt as if everything I had done in my life and especially every moment of my nature-writing endeavours had been as a kind of preparation for that moment, that moment when a humpback whale looked me in the eye, and it felt as if I had been sought out, chosen, the subject of a predestined moment. I had never known anything remotely like it before. I have never known anything remotely like it since.

And I have heard a humpback sing.

The boat engine was cut. The babble of our voices, edgy with adrenalin from an hour of watching the gamesomeness, the gay-foam-and-white-water making, was suddenly hushed. Sea sounds rushed in to the lull – wave slap, kittiwake cry, a flag that flapped in an easy breeze. For we were suddenly in among the whales, and a hydrophone was lowered over the side and connected to the boat's tannoy. We waited for the whales to sing. Breathe out, for heaven's sake. I breathed out. I thought it might sound a little like jazz, something Ellingtonian with Harry Carney on baritone sax, Cootie Williams on trumpet. Or, Coleman Hawkins on tenor sax playing *Solitude* unaccompanied has always seemed to me as a voice of nature, the breath of a haunted creature in the depths of night, or now that I thought of it, perhaps in the depths of oceanic gloom.

Or Sibelius: if anyone could write a score for humpback whale and symphony orchestra, he could.

Then it began.

Then my every preconceived reference point dissolved.

It began like wolves, then slid from high to a mid-register note, but then it stopped abruptly, which is not like wolves. Then a higher note, like a squeak (a second voice?), also cut off abruptly, a percussive interjection. Then a bass sound so low it warbled uncertainly among the limits of discernible notes. Then it began to rise as a second and third voice overlaid it, and suddenly Harry Carney was a valid choice and I felt elated, vindicated. Then silence, water sounds.

Then the repeats, a new version of– what had gone before, the song, the singing. I am a part-time musician but I have a full-time musician's ear, which I bent to what was going on. I heard rhythm, profoundly slow, but a constant pulse. Roger Payne said that whales give the ocean its voice.

THE OCEAN'S VOICE

Who taught you, Singer?
Who first caught your eye
and thought you fit to try out
a world-travelling song,
knowing your ways, bestowing
the pacific demeanour to navigate
between Alaska and Scotland?

And if I give you my
my most respectful silence,
my musician's ear and
my writer's best endeavour,
can you reach me, teach me
themes and variations,
cadences and nuances,

so that if I travel the earth
as you travel the girth of the ocean – singing,
I could be your tradition-bearer,
marry my voice to your song
and sing its worldly wisdom,
rhymes and all, to landlocked tribes
far from the ocean's thrall?

So why, when a humpback whale turned up and lingered for two months in the Forth estuary, and one of the best vantage points to watch it was but an hour's drive from my house … why would I respond with anything less than a euphoric flourish? No sooner have I posed the question than it occurs to me that I may have trouble answering it, for if truth be told my first reaction had rather surprised me too. In pursuit of an explanation then, let me first summon to my cause one William Topaz McGonagall, poet and tragedian, and the ghost of an old winter in my home town:

'Twas in the month of December, and in the year 1883,
That a monster whale came to Dundee,
Resolved for a few days to sport and play,
And devour the small fishes in the silvery Tay.

The events of that winter of 1883–84 in the Tay estuary off Dundee have long since been immortalised in McGonagall's poem, *The Famous Tay Whale*, which immediately became (and which remains) one of his greatest hits. He was an eccentric, perambulating, Victorian historic monument of Dundee streets. The "monster whale" was there at all because that autumn and early winter the North Sea had seethed with vast shoals of herring, and it lingered in the Tay because they were easier to catch in the shallower waters of the estuary than out at sea. Why the whale was in the North Sea at all was a mystery (as in 1883, so in 2017). Humpbacks prefer the oceanic scope of the Atlantic and the Pacific for their restless and more or less endless migrations up and down and across the globe. Our species names and pluralises and divides up the world's oceans to assist our own navigation and map-making, to give our land-masses geographical contexts. But humpbacks merely live in a single oceanic world. Visits to the comparative narrows of the North Sea are very rare events. The 1883 visit had consequences which, mercifully, did not – and could not – afflict the Forth's visitor in 2017. But back then there were the direst of consequences for the whale, and some time later, there were consequences for me. There are still consequences for me.

Dundee is where I was born and where I grew up, a city to which I still make many migrations every year. I love it dearly and it is still the only place I ever learned to think of as home. But it has a stain on its character, one which troubles a nature writer perhaps more than most of its natives. For around 170 years, beginning in 1752, Dundee was a whaling port. Eventually, in the late 19th century, it became the biggest in Britain. By that time, the whaling industry was diminishing all across Britain, but Dundee was also the global epicentre of the jute industry, and whale oil was in great demand there because it was perfect for softening the jute fibres. In the winter of 1883 then, the biggest whaling fleet in Britain was in its home port because the whaling grounds were out of reach in the winter. So when a humpback whale turned up, there were 800 whalers in Dundee with nothing to do.

The whale attracted huge crowds, made headlines. Local newspapers devoured its every move. The Edinburgh and Glasgow papers were hooked. *The Times* sent a man up from London. Whenever it appeared, whenever it put on a show, you could hear the cheers of the crowd at Broughty Ferry on the Dundee side of the river from two miles away, where a much smaller crowd would gather at Tayport on the Fife side. But the whalers wanted nothing to do with it. Then, after two weeks, during which the crowds – and the papers – had more or less relentlessly goaded the whalers to do *something*, the whale vanished. The crowds dwindled over the next few days, then they stopped coming altogether, and instead they set about polishing the whale's legend. For ten days, the firth was a blank page. If only it had stayed away, retraced its journey back up the North Sea into Norwegian waters then the great oceanic liberation of the Atlantic, it might have lived for another 150 years, swum a million miles, sired a new dynasty of humpbacks, added eight or nine tons to its weight, reaching around thirty-five tons. McGonagall would have been short of a poem and I would have been spared an uneasy inheritance. But after ten days, the whale came back.

The crowds redoubled, of course. They bayed for the thrill of the chase, and for two more weeks the whale swam and danced and sang. Still the whalers wanted none of it. They were enjoying not being at sea, a season of rest from the colossal labours of their trade. The shipowners were less than enthusiastic about rounding up crews to pursue a single whale in front of a crowd of thousands, a circumstance that reduced their dangerous deep sea trade to a game in the domestic shallow waters of the Tay. Almost certainly, they judged the humpback not worth the effort commercially. Its layer of fat is thin and yields very little of the precious oil, and it was well-known to whalers that the carcase of a harpooned humpback usually sinks. By comparison, the Greenland right whale's fat layer is thick and valuable, and it floats in death, hence right whale – the "right" whale to catch. So there was no commercial gain for the whalers. Even by the scant ethical standards of the day, there was no reason for that whale to die. The only people who wanted it were the crowds. And when the whalers did eventually give in, it was to indulge in nothing more than a blood sport, as blatant as a bullfight.

The hunt was farcical. It was hampered by all kinds of clowns in their boats who wanted a ringside seat. The whalers were probably a little ring-rusty, and their initial efforts were worse than useless. What followed was long, slow, inept, and no whale ever took longer to die than that one. Having been harpooned several times, it towed four boats far out towards the Bell Rock Lighthouse. The lines eventually snapped, the whale escaped, only to be found days later floating dead on the sea by fishing boats from Gourdon up near Stonehaven. They got ropes on it and towed it ashore, where the carcase was auctioned and eventually bought by a Dundee oil merchant. At which point, the humiliation of its life after death began.

To cut a very long story short, the whale was towed back to Dundee and its innards, including its skeleton, were removed. A kind of wooden skeleton and a great deal of stuffing restored it to something like a whale shape, and it was put on display with its mouth propped open (and in that open mouth were set a table and chair at which you could pose for a photograph, at a price). It then went on a tour of Britain by train, attracting massive audiences. Finally, the skeleton was donated to Dundee museum, where it is still on display to this day.

Nothing in nature, including being twenty paces from an adult grizzly bear in Alaska and being introduced to a captive wolf pack inside their enclosure in Devon, or even being temporarily trapped in a Cairngorms pinewood while rutting stags pounded and roared all around me … none of that has induced any semblance of fear in me. I am at my most tranquil in nature's company, and always have been. Except for my childhood encounters with the skeleton of the Tay Whale in the local museum. It was displayed by suspending it from the roof, and it is, of course, colossal. It was forty feet long when it was caught, and its tail measured seventeen feet and four inches across. When I wrote the whole story in a book called *The Winter Whale* (Birlinn, 2008), I remember that I lingered over that last statistic and considered the room in which I was writing at the time. I measured it, and it was a little over sixteen feet by thirteen. So the tail would not have fitted in the room.

The effect on my childhood self was that it haunted my dreams for a long time. I can't remember how long now, but it recurred again and again, one more grim consequence that the crowds and the whalers of my old home town never took into consideration in that winter of 1883–84 when the boats finally sailed and sealed the fate of the famous Tay Whale.

So …a humpback whale turned up in the shallow waters of the Firth of Forth in January 2017, and when the newspaper photographers and the TV crews turned up, not to mention squads of people with boats and cameras and phones and the internet at their disposal, I recoiled a bit and stayed away. There are no whaling fleets nearer the Firth of Forth than Norway, and in any case, the Norwegians only hunt minke whales. Times have changed. There were no crowds lining the shores; there were a few people with cameras and big lenses, binoculars and telescopes. I suppose the indifference is television's fault – what you might call Blue Planet Syndrome, where the perfection of the filmed sequences exceeds a thousandfold the expectations of what you or I might see walking the Fife Coast Path between Burntisland and Kinghorn on a squally, sleety day of an east coast winter.

But as it happens, I now have a unique souvenir of that particular humpback, thanks to my friend Leo Du Feu, a wildlife and landscape painter with whom I have shared the occasional book festival platform. Leo lives at Burntisland, so he did spend quite a few squally, sleety days walking and sitting still along that coast, making fast sketches (a talent of which I am more than a little envious) when the whale showed, and subsequently working them up into two oil paintings, one of which is facing me now on the wall of the room where I write. The image is a tranquil one, the whale breaking the surface in a dark curve that just reveals the "hump" and the small, pointed curve of the dorsal fin. The water is calm and bright (the viewpoint is south-facing), the whale at ease, which to my mind reflects the fact it was untormented by humanity throughout its stay. It left when it was ready to go, it suffered no wounds, it left no slick of blood in its wake, it towed no whaling boats out to sea; and given a fair wind it *will* live for another 150 years, and it *will* swim another million miles. I asked Leo if I could buy the painting because to me it represents a kind of reassurance. It is okay now to be a whale in the east coast waters of Scotland. Welcome. Thanks for coming and cheering our winter. We shoot only photographs. We have come a long way.

As for the Tay Whale skeleton, it has become the centrepiece of a new exhibition in The McManus (as Dundee's museum and art gallery is now known, named for the former Lord Provost Maurice McManus), although somehow the more sophisticated museum techniques of the 21st century have achieved a less threatening exhibit. In the autumn of 2017, the museum celebrated its 150th anniversary, an event it previewed with a specially commissioned wrap-round representation of the whale skeleton on the side of a double-decker bus. A newspaper photograph of the launch showed the bus and a group of boisterous, cheering and generally happy-looking Dundee schoolchildren, just about the age I was when the whale was giving me nightmares. That too is a kind of reassurance. If any of these children suffers in the way that I did at their age, and if one day they read this, my message to them is to hang in there, it will pass, and one day you may look a humpback in the eye and hear it sing.

Chapter Eleven

Jay is for Crow

ONE OF THOSE half-dark-at-noon days that January does so well moved sluggishly through the afternoon, fuelled by that lethargic species of rain that makes almost no sound but has the capacity to saturate in minutes everything and everyone in its path. It was falling when I was having breakfast, mid-morning coffee, lunch, mid-afternoon coffee (long sessions at the writing desk are punctuated with excuses for getting up and crossing the room to the kettle). It was an old January, and at the time my base was a kind of upstairs studio flat, an outpost of a hotel at the entrance to Balquhidder Glen. Just when I was thinking I needed the full-blown exercise of going downstairs to the bar, where I might have the day's first conversation with another human being, I glanced out of the window and saw pale light. The rain had stopped and the last hour before dusk promised to be the brightest – or rather the least dark – of the day, so I postponed the pleasures of the bar, stepped into wellies, grabbed a jacket and binoculars, and went out into the sodden world.

The nearest walking option from my desk was the forest that climbed the hillside behind my writing eyrie. It was a Commission forest, so not the most promising in wildlife possibilities, but the track would at least be firm underfoot whereas every other option would be sodden and soft, and in any case the object of the exercise on such a day is just to be out, to breathe clean air, and you just never know what might turn up.

The sky had just begun to lift from its base halfway down the hillside, a process that had the effect of draping the trees in thin scarves of cloud, as if the forest was smoking, although common sense would tell you that there are few circumstances less conducive to any kind of spontaneous combustion than such saturated windlessness.

Apart from my own footfall, a trickle of water in the ditch at the side of the track, and an occasional distant rumble from the main road far below, there was a conspicuous lack of sound. It was good to be out, but there was an unease about the forest in such a mood, and it communicated itself effortlessly into the mind of a solitary walker. Then the forest screamed.

As screams go, it was not so much a damsel-in-distress affair, more the conspiratorial screech of one of Macbeth's witches. There again, it appeared to emanate from high in the spruces, which would seem to rule out both damsel and witch. I spun round to face the source of the sound, at which point an answering scream sounded from the direction I had been facing, so I spun again, in time to catch a glimpse of the screamer as it threaded a buoyant and gently bouncing flightpath between trees. There was a flash of white, a hint of blue, a blur of tawny, another scream, then nothing at all.

The Gaelic name for it is *sgreuchag-choille* – screamer of the woods, which just goes to show how much the old

Highlanders knew about the creatures whose company they kept. The English "jay" is prosaic to the point of boredom, especially for such an un-boring bird. I had the idea of a silly children's book (a silly book for children, not a book for silly children) called *Jay is for Crow*, but before I got round to it, Helen Macdonald took the nature-writing world by storm with *H is for Hawk*, and that was that.

So I knew for sure that I was somewhere between two jays, whose last known locations were about 100 yards apart. Jays rarely stray far from their nest territory unless they run out of acorns, which is their favourite food, and paired-up birds rarely stray far from each other. But whatever these two were doing on this spruce-drenched hillside, they weren't looking for acorns. The chances are, I reasoned, they were a pair, and they would reappear sooner or later. I also reasoned that there was half an hour of usable light before darkness fell, that my chances of seeing anything more interesting were slim, so I may as well sit where I stood, lean back against this spruce trunk, and see if my reasoning bore fruit. Ten minutes (and four screams) later, there were ten jays on the forest track between twenty and fifty yards away from where I sat. Sometimes it just turns out that way, and you reap a modest reward because you made the effort to be out there and trusted the rest to instinct and stillness.

The birds appeared to be feeding, probably on beetles or spiders or some other forest floor bug lured into the open by the mild weather. The thing about the screaming, which is how you identify an invisible jay from quite a distance away, is that it's only the most obvious element in the jay's copious vocabulary. Sitting as close to them as I was, and with no other sights or sounds to distract either me or them, I was now treated to the collected works, as all ten birds kept up a sotto voce stream of chatter. The most frequent voice was a short, monosyllabic, flutey coo, which is not at all what you might expect. There were several variations on the theme of a crow-like caw, but shortened like soft explosions. There were also equally soft throaty chortles, both deep-voiced and falsetto, that reminded me a bit of my grandfather's pet budgie Joey, last seen lying dead in the seed tray about 1960, which is one of the more ludicrous images that my writer's mind has contrived on a Scottish hillside.

I then decided that there was also something of the budgie about the jay's exotic plumage: the pale, patterned head with the habitual raising of the small crown feathers into a "crest"; the black embellishments beneath the beak; the contrast of breast and back plumage; the black and white of wings and tail and the audacious flash of blue. It could easily be a fellow Australian.

Ten jays felt like a bit of a windfall. I decided they consti-tuted a winter foraging party, and that they had run out of acorns on their home patch, in which case they had done well to have found this corner of the Highlands. Jays like oakwoods because they like acorns, but they also like deep cover to nest and roost in, and the spaciousness of oakwoods does not supply deep cover. So if they can find an oakwood with, say, a spruce forest nearby, that suits them particularly well. And here was a spruce forest with oakwoods to the south and to the north (and I have seen jays in both), so perhaps it was not so surprising that I might stumble across such a midwinter gathering here. The fact that these were the first I had ever seen in that particular forest only reflects the secretive nature of many aspects of the bird's life. For despite its vivid plumage, its increasing willingness to take advantage of garden bird-feeders (if they're near oakwoods), and its so-conspicuous voice, it remains something of an enigma, and is extraordinarily accomplished in the art of not being seen when it chooses.

The restless gathering on the forest track suddenly took flight in a clamour of screams and a sparrowhawk looped down and sped after them. What happened next was infuriatingly concealed by towering banks of spruce, and all I can say with any certainty is that it was loud. But I now believe with complete conviction that the sparrowhawk was never born that could get the better of ten jays, for when it reappeared, it was in flat-out retreat down the forestry road and it was trailing a wake of ten screaming jays.

In the dead quiet that followed I eased myself up and out of what had been a very damp seat, and headed down into gathered dusk with the welcome destination of a room with a blazing fire and a glass of something distilled on a far Hebridean island for just such an occasion as this. It's a great country I live in.

◉ ◉ ◉

The rooks were singing with their mouths full.

If you have trouble with the concept of rooks singing at all, you probably have not spent time in a rookery on a mild day early in the year. Like most members of the crow family, rooks have a considerable repertoire. It is true that their most recognisable noise is the one that sounds like a donkey gargling, but they also make frequent forays into the falsetto territories of, say, Roy Orbison, although admittedly without the controlled vibrato or for that matter the perfect pitch. And when they do it with their mouths full of chunky twigs and broken branches during the nest-building season, it tends to sound more like Donald Duck than Roy Orbison. But they are singing.

An old countryman I used to know insisted that his neighbourhood rookery started nest-building on the first day of March. It was, he further insisted, as reliable as Christmas. He had watched it every year for forty years, he said. An old keeper had told him the date when he moved into the area, and year after year, so it had proved. Or so he used to insist. But I am far from convinced that the set-piece events of nature's year are ever as precise as that, and the old keepers whose paths I have crossed have tended to be strong on dogma and as inflexible as shotgun barrels. Or to put it another way, I don't believe a word of it. The rookery I know best is on the edge of Stirling, and is apt to dip a toe in the water of the nesting "season" as early as late December if the weather is mild enough, and take a break if and when the New Year turns seriously cold for any length of time. It's a common enough phenomenon in the bird world. Golden eagles are not the only ones to begin displaying, re-establishing territory, and renewing the pair bond around the turn of the year; they are quickly followed by ravens and herons, and I've seen Edinburgh's famous fulmars back at the nest ledge on Arthur's Seat in January.

The Stirling rookery is old and sustains several hundred birds, and these thicken the winter profiles of big beech, ash, oak and sycamore trees over several hundred yards. The trees throng the slope of a steep, east-facing bank that drops about a hundred feet. A small burn bisects the slope and provides the necessary doorstep water for the wood's badger sett. (I never yet found a sett that isn't near running water.) It's gloomy or downright dark in the heart of the wood on any winter day after mid-morning, although if there is late afternoon brightness in the overworld beyond the wood it filters through the topmost trees and brightens the high field beyond.

A mild day of midwinter is the best time to watch the rookery at work, and to eavesdrop on its raucous symphony. The sound of the more or less constantly opened throats of a hundred pairs of rooks requires a certain amount of scrutiny on the part of the listener before you get the sense of what's going on, of what underpins the harmonic structure of the symphony. I have no idea how long I have been listening, but it's quite a few years now, and I still haven't quite got the hang of it, but sometimes I think I'm making progress. I like to watch from a distance at first and from the sunny topside of the bank. The nests are all high in the trees and in clusters. Rookeries are sociable places, except that like most sociable places (pubs, for example), the sociabilities are punctuated by skirmishes. The territory of any one pair may only be a yard or so all round the nest, but they all seem to be vigorously defended. I am choosing my words carefully here: "seem to be" because of how often you see evidence of individuals clearing a space around the nest and keeping it clear. But it is a dangerous generality, for all that. With so many birds in such a relatively small area, it is pushing credibility to insist that all of them are equally adept and equally brave and equally bolshie when put to the test by their neighbours. As with almost any other species, you get smart rooks and stupid rooks, tough guys and timid guys, brazen birds and sneaky birds. It is not possible for all of them to behave identically, any more than it is possible that they all start nesting on the same day every year.

Rooks fly into the wood from every compass point carrying sticks, from skinny twigs to surprisingly hefty bits of branch. Watch the dexterity of the builder-bird as it grafts the stick into the growing structure and marvel, then watch the neighbours steal that very stick as soon as the builder has turned its back. As further evidence of character diversity, careful scrutiny reveals the accomplished thieves that never get caught and the hopeless ones that get a neighbourly rook beak in the side of the head for their trouble. I am tempted towards the idea that some rooks also have a sense of humour. Rook-watchers will get the most out of their day's work if they have one too.

The big winds of autumn always take their toll on such exposed nests, but whereas a much bigger treetop nest like, say, an osprey's, can be swept from the tree by a good gale, there is almost always something still in place when the rook begins rebuilding. New nests appear every year because first-time builders move in, but the older birds seem to return determinedly to the same nest year after year. Although that too is in danger of becoming an unreliable generality, there is anecdotal evidence at least (and some of it is my own) which suggests they are at the nest site so early in the year in order to reclaim their old nest. And like some carrion crows, there seems no doubt that some rooks repair and maintain their nests throughout the winter.

Between bouts of building, established pairs stand close together by the nest and croon to each other, a strangely affecting ritual to watch. It also comes as something of a shock that a rook, of all brash creatures, should reveal an intimate side to its character. The male also does a great deal of loud-voiced bowing to his mate as the nesting season progresses, a lusty, expansive gesture with overtones of aggression, but then he brings her food and offers it with manners of such delicacy that you find yourself smiling.

Now consider the individual bird itself as it stands on the topmost branch of a huge beech and contrives to catch the last of the sunlight, for it glitters glossy black and deep purple, an effect ever so slightly diminished by a pasty-white face and beak and a flashing black eye. The baggy-pants effect of the half-feathered legs also conspires to undermine further the glossy bravado. I was watching a rookery in Edinburgh once, wondering what the bird's full dress uniform reminded me of when it suddenly hit me – the Moderator of the General Assembly of the Church of Scotland wears breeches just like them. So I wrote the Edinburgh rooks a poem:

> *A very Edinburgh bird, the rook,*
> *Moderatorially cliquey;*
> *Black breeches and a grey look*
> *- Auld Breekie.*

I like to head down into the wood late in the afternoon of a rook-watching day and find a good tree to lean my back on, to sit for an hour in the gloom and watch with my ears. Once, I had been sitting for no more than about ten minutes, and had more or less readjusted my ears to the enhanced volume of the rookery from within, when it suddenly produced a roar that sped from one end of the wood to the other, and hundreds of birds took to the air at once. Three things produce that kind of reaction – a sparrowhawk, a buzzard or a peregrine falcon. A rook is ambitious prey for the hawk, and a buzzard is invariably more interested in rabbits when it crosses the rookery field, but when a peregrine spooks a whole rookery into the air, it has achieved the first object of the exercise and then tries to home in on one of the flying mob. Then it either chooses discretion rather than valour in the face of hundreds-to-one-against odds, or it pulls off something remarkable and there is a puff of black feathers. I was in the wrong place to see the cause of the unrest but the right place to feel the explosive nature of the mass launch. The unrest lasted well after the threat had passed. Birds circled noisily for several minutes, and even after most had resumed their stances at the nest, the havering was louder and angrier than before. So I guessed peregrine.

It becomes apparent when you sit beneath a rookery that the birds don't like the lower depths of the inside of the wood. It is, for example, littered with suitable nesting material. In fact, much of it is nest material dislodged by wind and weather from the previous year, but they leave it where it lies. Instead they forage far and wide in the brightness of day. I have never seen a rook on the ground inside the rookery wood. The nearest one I've seen from the inside of the rookery was perched on a gatepost just outside the upper edge of the wood. There, a long defunct gate reclined, attached to the post by a scrap of that phenomenon of human invention that binds the working Scottish landscape together the length and breadth of the land: blue baler twine. Rooks, like most crows, have a taste for bright or eye-catching stuff to decorate the nest, and this one had seen the blue baler twine flapping thinly in the wind. That twine must have been there for years, for the gate was worse than useless and the fence it used to serve is long gone, but that day that rook wanted that piece of twine.

I heard it before I saw it, a rhythmic drumming sound at odds with the unscored chaos of the rookery's symphony. I turned to pinpoint the sound and saw the rook on the post stabbing at the twine. This went on for quite a long time without any visible effect, then it perched on the gate and started to attack the knot. It put a foot on the twine to stop it moving and attacked it again with renewed zeal. It dropped onto a lower bar of the gate and attacked the knot from below. It yanked on one end, it yanked on the loop round the post. Then it looked as if it was trying to bite through the twine, then to saw through it.

Then a second rook appeared on the post and tried variations on the same theme. They worked as a team, hammering the twine against the post; they worked in opposition, tugging in opposite directions. A third rook arrived, remained for half a minute on the topmost bar of the gate watching the others at work then left. Perhaps it had offered advice.

The twine was still there when I left the wood. But when I returned a few days later, it had gone and the gate lay prone in the grass. I walked past the gate into the wood and there was the twine a couple of yards away. So what was all that about: a game? Or did it eventually weaken and fray beyond the point of no return after the rooks had given up and the burden of the gate suddenly became too much for the rook-weakened twine to bear? Alas, I will never know, and I feel bad about that. Perhaps if I had stayed for another hour ... ?

The rook in Scotland is mostly a Lowlander, thanks to its preferred feeding terrain, which is grassland, cereal fields, newly cut grass in public parks and even big gardens. Invertebrates, especially crane fly larvae and earthworms, and grain, are high on the list, but rooks never learned the more-or-less-anything-goes opportunism of carrion crows, jackdaws and ravens. The farmland of Aberdeenshire is something of a hotspot, and you'll find rookeries of almost 3,000 nests there, and a huge winter roost supplemented by Scandinavian birds. Many different species of birds flock in winter, of course, and vast numbers are not essential to create spectacle. A small birch full of goldfinches or waxwings has got enough vibrancy and colour and original design to make my day. And a dozen ptarmigan in level flight across the frozen shroud of Loch Coire an Lochain of Bràigh Riabhach will stay vivid in my memory for years. But when sixty thousand rooks take to the air at once and darken the sky and terrify your ears as if all the pipe bands of hell had struck up at once, then you are watching one of nature's truly great and truly inexplicable works. You watch, you listen, and your mind grows numb around a single question: what's it for?

But, of course, not every one considers such an eruption of birds as a wonder of nature. If you happen to be the farmer whose fields are in the path of the bird-lava as it descends, you have a different word for the rook. The printable version is "pest", for a winter rook roost on the march has a capacity to destroy young plants on a scale that is both impressive and – for the farmer – potentially disastrous.

Never having farmed, I don't know what the solution to that is, although it has always seemed to me that shooting out a rook's nest is one of life's more pointless acts of folly. But there have been endeavours in the matter of killing rooks on such a scale that they sound more like the campaigns of ancient Greek heroes – even Greek Gods – than anything even tangentially connected with agriculture. One of the most famous episodes in the history of rooks concerns one of the Earls of Haddington – or at least of his East Lothian estate workers – who, between the years of 1779 and 1793 killed 76,665. It is another of those improbably precise figures that punctuate the annals of some of natural history's more unnatural backwaters, and the answers to why the number is so precisely recorded, and what was so important about that particular span of fifteen years, have not been handed down with the numbers. I'm suspicious of all such routinely regurgitated accounts, but if you work on the no-smoke-without-fire theory, you will at least go along with the notion that here was a feat of rook-killing worthy of a Zeus, an Atlas, an Adonis, or even a Nemesis. The other conspicuously missing piece of information is whether or not it made any difference. It could just be that, in 1794, the Earl of Haddington abandoned his estate's rook-killing policy on the basis that it was a variation on the theme of farting against thunder.

Notwithstanding the earl's little local difficulty, it is undeniable – to a nature writer at least – that we would do better to accept the rook's often mesmerising contribution to the Lowland landscape of Scotland, to learn to live with and admire that winter eruption in our midst like a black fireworks display, to turn our finer feelings and an appreciative eye on nature's way of manipulating the landscape, whatever we as a species may want to do with it. Sooner or later, floods, wildfires and volcanoes go quiet and give us peace and time to rebuild until the next time. It's part of the price we pay for sharing the planet with all of nature's tribes. Sometimes it's just good to acknowledge that in addition to the many achievements of our species, we are still bit-part players in nature's greater scheme of things.

And if you ever wondered about the origins of the expression "bare-faced cheek", which we are apt to think of as the most audacious of human qualities, consider the young rook in his second year when he moults away his facial feathers, leaving that grey-white bare face that is the badge of all his tribe. The first bare-faced cheek of all, then, was the bare-faced cheek of the rook. So we're probably related. But we still sing better than they do.

◎ ◎ ◎

Suddenly the glen bursts free from its straitjacket of spruces into an open, sloping arena garbed in well-spaced, hand-planted, young Scots pines. You can tell at a glance which one nature prefers and I almost never disagree with nature.

Sunlight and snowlight smite you in the same instant and with an almost physical force, like benevolent winds. Waters pour down through mountain walls, churn and foam over falls, gather in the floor of the glen into common cause and head for Callander, which lies smoking frostily far below in the middle distance over your shoulder, beyond the spruces. All this I have drunk in greedily like one demented with thirst, thirst for high, bright, airy, wild places where ravens cavort and cough and chuckle in the blue-white airspace. For as long as I can remember, I have been that demented man.

It may only be February, but the ravens are already stroppily territorial, insufferable neighbours as usual, diving down at the head of a trotting fox on a dead-straight mission with his mate at its far end, roughing up a passing heron (which showed a surprising turn of speed in response), and generally making a spectacular nuisance of themselves. It seemed as if only I, of all the glen's creatures that day, was enjoying their presence.

There was so much light. The sun bounced off the high snow slopes above about 1,500 feet so that the male raven flashed glossy shades of inky blue whenever it burst out of shadow, a thing it seemed hell-bent on doing again and again in a series of rapid, turbulent circles from the lee of the darkest mountainside out into the open glen, each circle punctuated with hoarse, falsetto guffaws and short upside-down sprints, and swoops and climbs of such fluid grace and accomplishment that they flowed seamlessly into each other and levelled out again at the same circling height, a frenzy of deliberately eye-catching histrionics.

Somewhere nearby was his mate, watching in admiration (hopefully in admiration, otherwise what is the point of so much gleeful nonsense?) or pointedly fussing over the nest with her back turned, the subtext of that posture being that it is a fair distance from the corrie headwall to the nearest source of twigs, and further still (this being another Commission estate and therefore sheep-free) to find enough wool to provide a lining snug enough to thwart late-winter's blast. And time was marching on, and proper spring was waiting in the wings.

A kestrel was working the sunlit side of the glen, a shimmer of copper a-tremble on an airy stance, fan-tailed, black wingtips working sleekly in tandem with the wind, the head-down hunter of a nature writer's dreams and a short-tailed field vole's nightmares (it does occur to me from time to time that my presence in a wild landscape is at odds with almost everything else that moves there). It began to descend by jerky flights of uneven steps and landings, a pause on every landing, until it was no more than a dozen feet above the tops of the nearest pines, eyes intent on the slightest waver of mountain grass that might mean a vole losing its nerve and breaking cover.

Ravens do not approve of kestrels in this glen or anywhere else. The circling game that had been drifting in and out of the shadows and in and out of my mind, was suddenly abandoned in pursuit of a higher purpose. With wings half closed, the raven made a missile of itself, aimed itself at the kestrel and headed down a shaft of sunlight at speed, the archetypal hun in the sun. It was closing fast when the kestrel crash-dived feet-first into the grass. The raven pulled out a yard above and powered back up into the air, back-flipped at the end of its upward curve, completed the 360-degree roll with a second right-way-up flip and dived again. The kestrel saw it coming this time and sped away over the corrie floor, dodging through the pines more like a hawk than a falcon. The raven abandoned what had suddenly become a pointless pursuit, if indeed it ever had a point in the first place. It is often harder with a raven than any other bird to make out the blurred line between pointed aggression and pointless high-jinks-for-the-hell-of-it. It rose again in a long curve that took it back into the lee of the mountain then straightened out into a shallow climb aimed directly at the nest crag, where it landed and vanished among overhangs, boulders and shadows.

A bruise-coloured cloud was bearing down on the glen and the corrie out of the north-west, the unambiguous shade of snow in the offing. It announced itself with a series of icy flurries that soon thickened into draped curtains, curtains that hung in loose grey folds all across the headwall, yet the sun still shone and a species of airy sorcery began to transform the corrie's highest reaches. I put the binoculars on it just to watch the effect of the snow's dance among sunbeams, and slowly a snowbow began to arch palely across the whole headwall.

It seemed to have proved too much of a temptation for the ravens, for they suddenly appeared together high above the nest crag from where they charged the arch of the snowbow with a black counter-arch of their own. From my unique vantage point it was as if they had set out to burst the multi-coloured arch apart, to put a black breach in it, for there was a moment, as vivid in my mind's eye now as it was in

the flesh, when the two birds, not a yard apart, were a blaze
against the bow's bands of pale colour, so that it looked for
that instant as if they had broken it in two. And once was not
enough. They repeated the manoeuvre from different heights
and angles five times, and every time they dived down in a
curve, and if they were not mimicking the glorious curve
of the snowbow I don't what else they could possibly have
been up to. Each time they flew down, they burst the bow
apart as I saw it, but of course the bow would be advancing
before them as they flew, so they could not know they were
having that effect. But it did look as if they knew they were
mimicking the downward curve of the bow.

Snowbow and Ravens

There, where the bow crouched
between the forest and the falling snow,
so low it failed to touch the sky,
there, two ravens clad

in slicked-back glossy blacks, unfurled
their line astern attack that burst apart
the pale and the bright arcs, victory-rolled
and tally-ho-ed on down the valley,

where, shouting loutishly,
they failed to see the snowbow
heal itself behind their backs.

The snowcloud smoored the sunlight, and the snowbow
withered, faded away to that absolutely untraceable nothing
that only tricks of the light can achieve, the flakes thickened

and the snow began to reach down into the very depths of the glen. I edged into the lee of a rock to wait out the shower, for already I could see the far edge of the cloud where the sky was pale in the north. I wondered where the ravens went.

Then "Kruuk!" said a rock about twenty yards away, and there was a raven sitting on it that was not there seconds before, yet I had not seen it arrive. For perhaps two minutes I watched the snow touch down and melt on the bird's head and back, for it had turned to face into the wind and the direction of the falling flakes and with its beak pointing straight upwards, an attitude I had only ever seen once before – in whooper swans. The raven held that pose dead still until the snow stopped, and the irresistible conclusion was that it was enjoying the effect.

As the snow relented and the sun resumed, the raven shook itself like one emerging from a trance, scattering melted snow in droplets in a wide circle, croaked a second croak, leaned out into the wind on wide wings and lifted off into a low, slow glide like a hunting eagle, then curved out towards the middle of the glen again and surged forward into a shallow climb back up towards the nest crag and at once it was joined in the air by the second raven. For those two minutes I must have had two ravens perched within a few yards of where I sheltered, but I had not seen the first one arrive and I never knew the other one had been there at all.

There are salutary lessons at your disposal every time you go out into nature's company. This is a glen I know as well as I know anywhere. I know what to expect when I get there, and every time I leave again, what I take away with me is the lesson offered by what I did not expect. There is an intimacy at work between those creatures that live their lives here through every hour of the day and night and every season of the year. And in addition to the knowledge of the place that I have accumulated over the years, I also know this – that it does not amount to a thousandth part of the knowledge that lives on in the bird-brain of a raven. And if I live to be a hundred and I am still capable of walking up here, it would never once have occurred to me to play a game with a snowbow.

But my mind was bright and crackling with vivid images as I headed back downhill into the valley of the shadow of the spruces. An unkindness of ravens … whoever thought that one up was an idiot.

⊙ ⊙ ⊙

It was that hour of a midwinter afternoon my mother and her parents would have called tea time, which is to say any time after about a quarter to four. And for a quiet hour in an empty house I was sitting in my living room writing with a fountain pen in my hand and an A4 notebook in my lap. There are very few things in life I enjoy more or engage with more deeply than that wholly organic wet-ink-and-paper journey to the source of word-making. I had reached a bit of an impasse at the table where I usually work in the next room. So I switched off the laptop onto which I had been transcribing some handwritten notes, gathered up my thoughts and my notebook and pen, and migrated to a sofa to try and unfankle the knot in the only way I know how, which is by hand.

So I wrote by the soft light of a single table lamp, which was just about enough. I sat with my feet up so that I faced the bay window. It doesn't have what you might call a view, just a patch of sky above a dense thicket of trees and scrub, all of it constrained by the diagonal rooflines of two different houses across the road, so that the space between them is a wide inverted triangle. The thicket climbs a steep bank above a small burn that is unseen from the window. The trees were completely dark, unfathomable at that hour. They grow in two tiers, the thickly crowded bushy ones just above the burn, then the taller and more spaced out trees at the top of the bank where the sun can get at them. In midwinter, their bare branches are etched against the sky.

For much of that hour, then, I had been unconscious of the world beyond the window. My eyes, like my heart and mind, followed the pen's smooth journey across the page, the slow stitching of a word garment the page will wear for as long as the notebook survives. I am a relentless chucker-out of things, so we are not talking about immortality or archives here. It will be lucky to survive a year.

I made progress. The knot began to loosen. Then something caught the corner of my eye and I looked up. There was a new moon high up in the window, not only that but the space below the moon and above the trees was full of jackdaws flying from right to left across the window in a ragged but more or less constant procession of squadrons from a handful at a time to fifty or sixty at a time. Their destination was obvious. A mile away in that direction is the rookery wood, part of which serves as the jackdaws' winter roost.

That midwinter-to-late-winter "tea time" hour embraces the last of the light and it embraces jackdaws. It has become my jackdaw hour too, for they have more or less ritualised the procession. The flight is never less than playful. Sudden scrums break off from the mainstream, run through a few manoeuvres of roughhouse aerobatics, then rejoin the general southward progression towards the wood.

For the moment then, the writing hand was still, and I watched the window's meagre ration of sky. In its lowest understorey it lured a yellow tint, which crept across the window from the sunken sun in the south-west. It spread and intensified over a few minutes, firing up the light behind the bare branches. But it faded as the moon brightened, and that higher band of sky eased away from that palest of pale blues (a shade which momentarily recalled the day-long shade of the snow on Beinn a' Chrulaiste; it belongs exclusively to late winter and no other fragment of nature's year) to an almost colourless silver. Considering it was my living room window and a quiet street on the edge of Stirling, it was briefly and surprisingly beautiful.

And all the time until the sky was truly black, the jackdaws sped by, and in my head I supplied the soundtrack that never lets up when jackdaws are on the move, and which sounds like ricocheting bullets in a good western film, or so I have always thought.

Then, at the darkening, a star came and pinned itself to the sky just to the right of the moon, and that changed everything, for suddenly my mind's eye was not seeing a skyscape that had just emptied of jackdaws but a work of art. For such a moon and such a star in just such a juxtaposition were the most recurrent motifs in the works of George Garson, a device which was in turn his own homage to one of his artistic gods – Samuel Palmer. For his 70th birthday, his wife Jean had somehow found a small Palmer etching, a rural landscape with a crescent moon and a star, and for those last ten years of his life, he kept it more or less within touching distance.

In my own family, such a moon is known affectionately as a Garson moon, for it adorned his letters, cartoons, cards, hasty sketches, one beautifully worked large pencil drawing, finished paintings, and one small slate mosaic, and in one way or another his love of the very image that now stole into my window touched us all.

I don't have tea at what my mother used to call tea time any more. But sometimes it coincides with the end of a long writing shift and I pour a small whisky. As it happened, that tea time of the jackdaws and the moon and the star was one of those whisky moments. The whisky happened to be Orcadian, which was accidentally and happily appropriate, and the water I splashed into the glass came from a plastic bottle I had filled from the snow-fuelled burn in the raven's glen under the mountain. I raised my glass to the ghosts of Salmuel Palmer and George Garson, to the free-flying tribe of jackdaws, and to the sense of well-being I recognised when all three decided to drop in on me unannounced one late afternoon at the end of winter.

Chapter Twelve

A Diary of Late Winter

Two MILES WEST of Stirling, a discreet forest track slips away uphill from a quiet backroad, climbs and hairpins its way up the north-facing slopes of a low range of flat-topped hills. These define the valley of the Upper Forth on its southern side, the fertile flat-bottomed fields of the Carse of Stirling. Forestry operations have clear-felled the lowest slopes, and in the process they have opened out one of the most revealing insights into the fundamentals of Scottish landscape.

Right in front of me, right in the middle of my panoramic view in which Lowlands tilt deferentially northwards towards Highlands, and exactly at my eye level about 200 feet above the Carse, two buzzards worked along the newly revealed slopes and the near edge of sunlit fields. They flew slowly in independent but constantly interconnecting circles, one sunwise, one widdershins. From time to time they called to each other, that plaint, that down-curved glissando through a minor third, kind of bluesy. Miles Davis would have liked it. And Stan Getz. Something in the languorous curves of flight and flight-call and the loosely coiled river far beyond them seemed to me to make companionable, harmonic sense, as if they were aware of each other and agreed for that tranquil and sun-smitten moment to move to a common rhythm. It amazes me how often the moods of jazz and nature evoke each other. I wonder why jazz has not made more of the phenomenon down the years. There again, any inspection of the lifestyles of jazz music's defining stylists is not going to reveal too many students of nature.

I homed my binoculars in on the female buzzard. For the moment, her mate had moved further east and drifted behind me towards the edge of the standing timber higher up the hillside, but she held up into the north wind, paused there dead ahead of me and hung for a few seconds, then eased out of that airy stance to draw a level figure of eight. She repeated it three times as if she was trying to scratch it deeper into a flat disc of space. Whenever her curving flight brought her round to face the hillside, she revealed herself as what ornithology calls a "pale phase" bird, her breast almost white but with a scarf-like band of pale brown. Buzzard plumage is a thing of almost infinite variations on a theme of brown and cream and off-white.

She began to rise, resumed a circling flight, until she had placed herself on the sky just above the easternmost summits of the long arc of mountains that so defines this landscape, the unmistakable signature of the Highland Edge. She locked herself into a series of sunwise circles, five of them, wide and dead level, and not for the first time in my life I envied the buzzard's perspective of this landscape. With her leisurely, head-down scrutiny, she knows every curve and hidden fold of the river, and with her careful level scrutiny of the horizon, she knows the pageant of mountains as I never will. At that moment she read my mind, abandoned the fifth circle and set off due west in a straight-winged glide, and as I followed her in the glasses the mountain roll call drifted through the lenses ... Ben Vorlich, Stuc a' Chroin, Beinn Each, Ben Vane, Ben Ledi, Stuc Odhar, Ben Venue and, most westerly of all, Ben Lomond. These are the front rank of the mountains, the ones which define the Highland Edge, the ones which signifiy to buzzard and buzzard-watcher that beyond them all is changed; there be dragons. Behind these, dropped hints of others lurk, some higher and whiter ... Ben Chonzie, Ben More, Stob Binnein, the Arrochar hills beyond Loch Lomond including the Cobbler, Beinn Ìme, and another Ben Vorlich. High pressure had begun to build, the sky was clearing following yesterday's heavy mountain snow then rain. The mountains still held some of the snow, but their rivers would be convulsed with meltwater. The sun was strong in the middle of the day, but with the wind out of the north, it offered no warmth.

The buzzard wheeled far to my left and retraced her flight, going east now, the order of the mountains reversed as she flew. She came past me about a quarter of a mile out over the fields, and there her mate reappeared rising from below her and fell in with her, darker and more compact, and he led her on a wide curve of flight that leaned out against the pale gold of Sheriffmuir and the long eastward sweep of the Ochil Hills.

South of the Ochils, two ancient volcanic plugs almost close the valley of the Forth, but the river has always plied a snaking course between them, shaping not just the lie of the land but a thousand years of the history of the whole country. The more southerly of those volcanic plugs accommodates

Stirling Castle, the other the national monument to William Wallace. Both were carefully sited to be visible for many miles, from flat fields, from surrounding hills, from the mountains. It is, it has always been, a landscape to be reckoned with.

A kestrel slipped discreetly into the airspace they had vacated. I am convinced that the kestrel's decline and the buzzard's new prosperity are not coincidental, that the one prospers at the expense of the other. The Carse still holds a fair number of kestrels, but the buzzards outnumber and out-muscle them and they have to work harder than ever for their living. The buzzards have even found niches inside Stirling itself, where they give the grey squirrels a hard time of it.

This kestrel faced the mountains and the north wind. Its dialogue with the wind was always much more fluent than the buzzard's. The sun lit it from above and behind with a fetching coppery sheen that shimmered as the bird hovered. I climbed with the track as I watched it, and at first it was above me, then at eye level, then below me, as it navigated the airspace in vertically downward intervals to a new hovering perch on nothing at all. After the buzzards, this was an utterly different approach to the same landscape, and thanks to my own elevated stance on the hillside, something of the possibilities of flight stole into a corner of my mind.

Then, in a stacked pile of wood that was nothing more than smashed fragments of felled trees, a wren emerged from its nearest edge and perched there, blinking in sunlight (it must be gloomy inside such a woodpile). It whispered a few syllables to the wind, then scudded a few yards towards the heap's northern end, and having risen no more than a single vertical foot, disappeared again into its woody sanctuary. That too was one of the possibilities of flight.

◉ ◉ ◉

Two days later, far out among the fields of the Carse, the snow all but gone from the mountains, the river looking bloated, pools of standing water in the stubble fields, and the light in the early afternoon had a strange silvery quality. There was an alacrity in the air as if nature had tired of winter already and wanted to get on with the year. I had paused to watch two large flocks of birds that had just alighted in the same field. One was mostly the Scandinavian thrushes – fieldfares and redwings, about 300 of those, I guessed; the other was a mix of finches, yellowhammers, siskins, corn buntings, linnets, and goodness knows how many there were of them. As they fed, they seemed to establish a kind of no man's land in the middle of the field, with the thrushes on the far side of it and the finch-sized birds closer to the single-track farm road and its fringing hedges.

The birds were clearly nervous. They knew better than I that, sooner or later, such a gathering of so many small birds in a single field was bound to attract the attention of a predator. At every small or substantial alarm, as small as a dog bark and as large as a snorting tractor on the road, the finch flock fled to the hedges and filled the air with their voices. A shudder went through the thrush flock as they stopped to assess the threat then fed on. The finches poured back into their portion of the field and fell silent. Then there was a fox in the field.

I saw it first just as a patch of colour in the furthest corner. There is a small wood over there, then a deep and steep-sided ditch and a fence and a hedge, and if the fox had come from the wood it must have negotiated all three. There was a thin strip of longer grass by the hedge and the fox was there, half in and half out, dead still, assessing the possibilities. It was a big field, the fox had at least fifty yards of open ground to the nearest bird. I had expected a flat-out sparrowhawk or peregrine, not this dead-slow-and-stop stalk in the long grass. But no bird flinched.

Except one. That one was a heron of all things; it appeared from somewhere beyond the corner of the wood, all wings and dangling legs, homed in on the fox and screeched, the way herons do when they are discomfited by pretty well anything. The fox turned in its own length and vanished beneath the hedge. The air above the field convulsed. The finches exploded up from stubble to hedge, a low-level, high-voltage retreat. But the fieldfares and redwings rose in silence and flew in disciplined order to a pair of tall ash trees, one each side of the road, and suddenly the bare branches were thickly clustered with a foliage of thrushes. I turned back to the far corner: the heron stood precisely where the fox had been.

Then I realised that the whole episode had been watched by a buzzard, huddled and fluffed up on a telegraph pole, and in that bulked-up form and from behind, it had the look of a crouching eagle. I decided to move on, edged the car towards the buzzard's pole. It put up with me creeping slowly past, but as soon as I stopped it stepped off and glided down to a yard above the ground, crossed the field beyond, then rose again to another pole a hundred yards away. There it perched side-on, fluffed its feathers again, trapping a cushion of air with which to fend off the north wind, and held its wings loose and unfolded, like a compact eagle. I was intrigued because it had not flinched when the fox and then the heron and then the small bird chaos intruded on its afternoon. It didn't even seem to be watching. Perhaps it was as simple as this: it had a specific prey species on its mind, vole most likely, and it was watching a known vole terrain (it carries that kind of knowledge the way you or I know where the good cafés are). Or perhaps it was even simpler: it was well fed, it was tholing a cold winter afternoon, and there was nothing on its mind at all.

Late in the afternoon I edged my car down the rough access track to Flanders Moss, a regular haunt towards the south-west corner of my working territory, and a few miles to the west of the buzzard pole where the flat fields of the Carse run out and give way to wetland and forest and the land starts to curl up at the edges towards the foothills of the Highlands. The Moss used to be a reliable winter roost for hen harriers, but in the early decades of the 21st century, nothing at all about hen harriers is reliable. They still turn up, but they are few and far between. For that matter they are few and far between everywhere on the face of the land, and we have the grouse moor industry to thank for that.

The mountains had dragged new snow showers across their south-facing slopes, but low sunlight carved an eerie wedge of yellow light across the foothills and only the foot-hills, for it neither glanced off the falling snow nor flooded over the wide sprawl of the Moss, which lay robed in its own mysteriously tea-shaded shadow of winter heather and winter grass. Its hundreds of watery patches and its puddles, pools and ponds reflected no colour of any kind, yet there was an unearthly beauty in its utter colourlessness, a very rare thing in nature. There were pine marten scats on the path.

I followed the edge of a birch wood to the south-east corner of the Moss where the birches form a containing right angle. From here, the Moss offers the widest horizon in all the land of Menteith. Only lochs normally have this kind of spaciousness, but in the wider Trossachs area they are all hemmed in by forests, hills and mountains. The Moss is like a huge wheel laid flat on its tabletop of water and moss and heather and peat with only a thin "tyre" of rimming trees. The foothills and the mountains lean back and keep their distance.

In the last of the light I climbed the reserve's observation tower on the off-chance that a harrier or two might slip in under cover of dusk. I was just halfway up when I saw a harrier-shape through the timber spars of the tower. By the time I reached the top, it was not in sight. What I had seen was a female, which is to say it was brown, and in that light and against that bog-at-dusk background, the chances of finding it again diminished by the second. I simply scanned the land with the glasses, moving slowly from south to north and from east to west, hoping against hope of catching something which looked like a piece of the Moss that had taken flight. And that was exactly what I found, and for about twenty seconds and at the very furthest edge of reliable vision I saw its impossibly slow flight, its wingtips just inches above the ground, the white blaze at the base of its tail occasionally showing up to confirm that it was what I thought it was. Then it passed behind a screen of small birch scrub and I didn't see it again.

Every time I see a hen harrier out here, which is not often, or up on a quiet corner of the Ochil Hills, or above the trees at Glen Finglas, I am reassured to this extent, and this extent only: it's one more hen harrier that has slipped through the net, one more that those who like to "manage" nature with a shotgun in one hand and a dose of poison in the other have not yet shot or poisoned or otherwise removed from the face of the land.

◎ ◎ ◎

The blizzards charged eastwards across the land, leaving the mountains breathless and beautiful for a day or two. Then the temperature rose, the rains came, it grew too mild for anyone's winter comfort … by the end of January it had become an erratic pattern, a predictable sequence of events. Not even the rains set in for long, and the fitful appearance of watery sunlight became a kind of default setting, so that from time to time and day after day, the sodden land was briefly ablaze where the sun bounced and dazzled from every imaginable form of standing, running and dripping water. I lived in wellies, I ploughed a four-wheel-drive furrow around the backroads most afternoons, squelched among woods and fields and foothills in search of swans and foxes, hares and deer, river otters, restless and bewildered shoals of birds; and as I ploughed and squelched I tried to piece together a sense of how nature was facing up to this too-warm, too-spasmodic winter, writing down whatever turned up.

There was one upside to the whole chaotic mess: rainbows.

Seared in my mind even now is a moment when I had just clambered back into the car after a long wander by the river and the discovery of a family group of six mute swans finding the swollen current hard going. There can be few stronger swimmers in the bird world than mute swans, but again and again their attempts to make headway upstream failed and the cob would urge his brood up onto their feet then into a wave-thrashing, feet-pounding, running flight on the surface of the water, and in that way they would cover fifty upstream yards before subsiding back onto the surface, at which point they were once again incapable of headway. The process was repeated again and again, while I scratched my head trying to understand why they didn't just fly, or get up on the bank and walk. I don't know how long I watched, but when I eventually plodded back to the car and clambered in, started the engine, edged forward from a watery verge onto the road, I was no sooner mobile than something astonishing filled the driver's door mirror. I reversed the few yards I had just driven, grabbed a camera, and jumped out. Wedged between the bottom of the Ochil Hills and the Wallace Monument on its wooded rock was a fat lump of rainbow.

Not only was the sun very low, but it was working on two fast-moving showers of rain about a mile apart. One consequence was a double rainbow, but the main arch was also of a double thickness. Where the pot of gold should have been, between the monument and the hills, was one of the showers, and it was lit gold. It was that point of colli-sion between the rainbow's double-thickness arch and the lit rain that produced that fat wedge of saturated rainbow colours, and even as I watched it, it contrived a ghostly twin image of itself.

Then, as the gold shower moved on towards the east, it had a curious effect on the base of the rainbow, as if it was nibbling into it from the edge so that from time to time, bits of the rainbow were missing. The arch had vanished, so that there was only this leaning-over wedge towering over the monument. The spectacle was as bizarre as it was beautiful, and it produced a somewhat bizarre response, for I suddenly had the notion of a colossal rainbow-shaded tree trunk being gnawed at by a golden beaver. I stood and stared and stared, and as nature-as-sorcerer went through its paces I started to laugh at the joy and the wonder and the sheer madness of it all.

⊙ ⊙ ⊙

Snow was promised by breakfast. I had heard this before on a dozen different weather forecasts, and none of them had delivered, at least not in my neck of the woods, not below about a thousand feet. I woke at four in the morning, peered round the curtains at a white street and heavy snow falling in a big wind. Oh joy. By breakfast time the sun was out of course, and although snow showers punctuated the morning they had already lost their fervour and I felt cheated again. But it was the first time in four years I had needed to select four-wheel drive to get out of the street, so that was something.

I travelled the Carse by its wee roads, and the Ochils and all of the lower hills were white, the fields were white, the wee roads were white. The mountains were lost, still snowing up there behind and beneath those piles of grey-black clouds. Birds were on the move everywhere, homing in on the stubble fields in huge numbers. The fieldfare and redwing flock had doubled in size in a few days, likewise the masses of small birds. Everything on the ground faced into the north-east wind. Everything that flew in over the hedges would reach a point in the field where they would wheel through ninety degrees, stall and land … facing the same way as the rest. The feeding was conspicuously frantic, and it became clear that it was being plundered between brutal showers when the sky darkened, the wind (and the wind-chill) picked up, and everything bolted for cover. It evolved into the most restless of days. The weather was restless, the sky was restless, the birds were restless. Clouds tore along hillsides and packed themselves thicker and thicker against the mountains. The sun shone and vanished, shone and vanished. The moon arrived and stood over Stirling Castle, and vanished, and so briefly did Stirling Castle, briefly obliterated from its ancient stance, a feat which was never accomplished by English kings and Oliver Cromwell.

Sitting in the car, watching through an open window, I felt like the still centre of the wild world, as if I should be doing more. But my job was this. As one more shower thudded into the car, the hedge five yards away filled up with tree sparrows and linnets, and they burrowed deep inside it and gossiped loudly for every moment of the deluge. Then the sky lightened, the wind calmed, the sun stole out, and they were gone. Then suddenly everything was restored at once. The sun and the wind started to bore into the mountain clouds, making holes just above the foothills but never quite revealing the summits. Geese piled in, adding to the mayhem in the stubble fields, and perhaps they had been waiting out the storms on the river, keeping their heads down below the level of the highest banks. A big flight of rooks drifted over, sounding like heavy agricultural traffic, and launched dozens of dummy-run assaults on a solitary kestrel on a fence post. It finally tired of them and headed west, and so did I.

Out near Flanders Moss I found it again – on a fence post, being harassed by jackdaws. I had stopped to watch, but then I found my attention distracted by some odd shapes in the field across the road. They were dark and inert, they looked like sods of earth where the snow had melted (except that the snow had not melted), or lumps of spread dung (but there was no spread dung). The field had been partly ploughed before the snow came, and the shapes lay in the hollows made by the plough and partly filled in by the snow. None of them moved, and yet there was something about them that did not quite make sense. Nothing else in the field was free of snow. I reached for the binoculars and what snapped into focus was a flock of lapwings. But they were so hunkered down that only the broad dark curves of their backs and the slim curves of their crests showed.

A single sentry bird got to its feet. Otherwise, not one bird moved, this despite my very obvious presence standing by my car and my very obvious interest in them. The field at my back, which the kestrel had just crossed, seethed with jackdaws, sparrows and starlings. The field where I had stopped earlier was feverish with birds. All across the Carse, that winter bird highway thrummed with traffic. Yet there, thirty yards away, these lapwings were still enough to make me think at first glance that they had been sods of earth. It was three o'clock in the afternoon, the sun was out, there were two hours of usable daylight, followed by a long, cold night. Why were these birds and these alone not making hay while the sun shone?

They had the look of birds that had just reached journey's end after migration, probably from somewhere down the east coast, Northumberland perhaps. Behind them was a journey up the coast, into the Firth of Forth, then the long haul upstream. If you make such a journey, this is as far inland as you can get in this part of Scotland. Keep going west and you run into the mountains, and you start to close in on the long sea lochs of the west coast. Go north from here and its mountains all the way to Orkney. This was journey's end all right. If I'm right, these lapwings migrated about six weeks early. So, were they lured by an absurdly warm December and an all-but snowless January? Nothing more than dropped hints of winter, a day or half a day at a time while the temperature swithered between ten and fourteen degrees. Is this, in other words, another symptom of climate change convincing enough to tamper with one of their most fundamental biological functions; convincing enough to delude them into migrating six weeks early, only to find that winter had turned up on the day they arrived? Can that happen? Yes, it certainly can. Was it happening right there in front of my eyes? I don't know. But I think so.

When I left them, I drove on to Flanders Moss (finches, linnets, geese and jackdaws again, wrens a-twitch everywhere in the woods). When I passed the lapwings again more than an hour later, it looked very much as if not a single bird had moved. In all that time, the sun had shone. That night, there was an almost full moon at the end of my street, the temperature had dropped below zero, and then it had started snowing again.

Three days later it had thawed again, the temperature rose in a day from minus five to plus ten, the snow was gone from the fields and the low hills and the mountains wore stripes. I went out in the early afternoon and found the kestrel again in the same place but on a pole rather than a fence post. I pulled in to watch from a distance, saw it follow a line of poles down the side of a farmhouse track. It perched halfway to the farmhouse, despite the hover-friendly breeze out of the west. Twice within five minutes it dived straight down into the grass verge by the track and twice returned empty-taloned to the same perch. Then it tried a third perch much nearer the farmyard. I saw now there was a ruined outbuilding behind the house, and I suspect that might be where it nests when the time comes.

Out of idle curiosity I scanned all the fields that I could see, and counted all the poles that were available to a hunting kestrel. Over about half a square mile there were more than fifty. Now how might that change the characteristic hovering behaviour of the same hunting kestrel? It flew suddenly in a shallow, flat-out dive that covered hundreds of yards before I lost it. I turned back to the farm track in search of an explanation. I found it: there was a buzzard low over the field and coming from the direction of the kestrel's last pole. It flew slowly, carrying hefty prey. It perched on a fence post and began eating at once, but it looked up often in the direction the kestrel had taken. Once again, I was wondering about the impact the proliferation of buzzards has had on kestrels. Thirty years ago, there were more kestrels and no buzzards here. A final thought on the subject: in a previous life, I commuted from Stirling to an Edinburgh newspaper office early in the morning, and I used to count kestrels at the side of the M9. My record for one journey of about thirty miles was fourteen. Now, if I have cause to drive to Edinburgh, I see no kestrels, but I do see buzzards.

And while I am rounding up final thoughts, I left the buzzard and drove west to the field where I had seen the lapwings. More of the field had been ploughed in the interim, but the lapwings were still there, feeding in the stubble, but no more than twenty yards from where I had first seen them. So I had cemented one more small theory about climate change securely into place.

⊙ ⊙ ⊙

Airthrey Loch on the campus of the University of Stirling is a swan water. All kinds of wildfowl use it, but it is owned by mute swans, or more specifically one mute swan, the resident cob. I have spent more hours watching swans than any other creature, and more hours writing about them. I have watched them all across Scotland, from Shetland to Solway and from the Western Isles to the east coast. And from Lindisfarne to Norfolk to a swan hospital in Surrey. And trumpeter swans in Alaska, and whooper swans nesting on an Icelandic beach of black volcanic sand with the volcano in question – Hekla – for a backdrop. Over the years, I have learned among many other things to avoid generalising and to recognise individuality. I have met clever swans, stupid swans, brave swans, timid swans, reasonable swans, unreasonable swans, enlightening swans and downright baffling swans. I have yet to find a swan that turns into a beautiful swan maiden, but I haven't finished looking yet.

And sometimes you come across the mute swan cob from hell. Airthrey Loch has such a cob. To begin with, he is huge. They always are. He is also fearless. They always are. And when he does that thing that all swans do, "standing" on the water with head and neck held high and wings flourished and wide open so that they crack like sails in a big wind, it becomes a gesture intended to intimidate, and it succeeds. When he strikes that pose on still water so that it reflects itself and becomes an exquisite, two-headed, four-winged monster, it becomes difficult to overstate the impact. I have tried to imagine how that must look to a lesser swan or a mere duck or a swimming otter down at water level, and I think it must look as if the Celtic gods have moved in to terrorise all lesser beings.

Winter is a difficult time for swans, especially young swans in their first year. The mortality rate is exceptionally high. Some adults pairs look after their brood right through the winter and only evict them from the territory when they start entertaining nesting notions again. Other parents throw them out before winter sets in. Airthrey's cob is one such parent. Luckily for his offspring, the loch is effectively two lochs connected by a long narrow middle section. The larger of the two watersheets is owned by the cob and his mate, the smaller is where the banished offspring go, and there they can winter well enough, for their water is sheltered, there is good feeding both in the water and on large areas of mown grass. The reliable presence of humans with handouts also helps.

On a day towards the end of winter, with a fair bit of ice on the surface of the smaller loch and the narrow connecting stretch, I had wandered that way with a camera and my insatiable swan curiosity. The cob was already well fired up, and was clearing everything from coots to goosanders to geese from his path in a series of fast swimming charges with neck furled, head held low and wings hoisted like mainsails. Some of these sallies evolved into wing-thrashing lunges, his colossal black webbed feet and his wingtips thrashing the surface with fear-inducing rhythmic precision. So far, so predictable. Then I heard the wingsong of more swans in flight. If you ever had a humming top as a child and you remember the noise it made, and if you can imagine that sound broken up into rhythmic four-in-the-bar fragments, that is the song of a mute swan's wings in flight, a pulse of extraordinary beauty. When its echo bounces back off the frozen surface of a winter loch, then you know for sure you are eavesdropping on the language of one of nature's chosen tribes.

Three swans came low over the loch, undercarriages lowered, wings angled and gliding, but at the last moment they pulled out and went round again, and if the change of mind was instigated by the sight of the cob in full flow, they failed in that one moment of doubt to appreciate the full implications of what awaited them. For they circled again, and this time they landed on the water and by the time the water around them had subsided, the cob was twenty yards away and closing. Fast.

In this mood of more or less constant belligerence, nothing heightens it to a pitch of terrifyingly concentrated rage like the arrival of a new adult swan. And now there were three of them. As often as not, a cob's territorial sallies are designed to deter, to deliver a sermon about discretion and valour and all that. Physical contact is comparatively rare. What followed was all physical contact. After the first lunging assaults, two of the incomers fled. The third was either a little slow on the uptake or it was made of stronger stuff and was in the mood for a challenge. But this was David facing up to Goliath in a version of the story in which Goliath hadn't read the script. He first grabbed a beakful of the smaller swan's back and held on. The victim let out a yelp that could only be pain. Then he was simply unable to free himself as the sheer weight of the assailant bore down on him. Then the attack moved to the neck, and at every bite the victim yelped again and again. Finally, the cob drove his victim against the bank and then the attack really got going. How this might have resolved itself is not a pleasant speculation, but there was a fisherman on the bank, and he, brave soul, waded into the water, separated the swans and stood between them. He was a big man, over six feet and well built, and the cob didn't give a damn. He eluded the fisherman's defences and time after time he charged again at the swan on the bank, always going for the neck, always inflicting pain. But the fisherman hung in there and finally succeeded in ushering the injured bird far up the grass bank, at which point, honour more than satisfied, the cob withdrew a few yards on to the water, where he was joined by his mate, and they rose on the water together, flourishing their wings and calling loudly, as blatant a demonstration of triumphalism as you will ever see in nature.

Some swans are better at the "nuclear option" school of territorial rule than others. Here, it works. There are six very healthy-looking young swans on the smaller part of the loch, the cygnets from last summer, and now, at the end of their first winter, with the brown plumage of their nursery months giving way to their first coat of brilliant white, they look primed, ready to go out into the world, where it is just possible they will join forces with the seven cygnets that flew from here last year. Demonstrably, they have wintered well. Demonstrably, their parents know what they're doing, and any day now they will finally clear their offspring from their nursery waters, forcibly if necessary.

Chapter Thirteen

Insh Marshes: A Waterworld with No Half Measures

THE LONGER THE NIGHTS, the more precious the daylight. At the latitude of the Insh Marshes in the upper reaches of Strathspey and the lee of the northern Cairngorms, December rarely doles out more than six usable hours of the stuff. Between dawn and dusk, the daylight fliers cram the hours with hunting. These are the dark days, which the weak and the ill-starred rarely survive. At this time of year the Insh Marshes are a waterworld with no half measures, as uncompromising as Iceland, which may be why Icelandic whooper swans feel at home here. Their beauty and their arctic-toned music dignifies every Strathspey winter. Wetlands this expansive, this wide-open, this wild, are the stuff of nature's own dreams, and it is not possible to overestimate their value.

There should be beavers here. In nature's scheme of things, such a wetland should be aided and abetted and managed and manipulated by beavers, because their presence is capable of increasing the biodiversity of such a landscape fourfold, so it becomes four times as priceless.

The marshes lie between two of the Highlands' set-piece

mountain massifs, the Cairngorms to the east, the Monad-hliath to the west, and every December the snow unfurls down their flanks by degrees, according to the depth of winter, the one in shadow when the other is in sunlight. It is a sorcerer's landscape. Birch woods, garbed in that mysterious winter purple that stows away their tight-packed finery of the seasons to follow, climb up and over low ridges between here and the Cairngorms' pinewoods. They also offer cover for a nature writer on a mission. Mostly when I have come here at this time of year my priority has been the swans, but I have also come in hope of renewing another old acquaintance.

An hour drifted by, drifted from one woodland-edge viewpoint to another, to another, to another ... each one opening out a different portion of the marshes, a different set of possibilities. A little elevation goes a long way on the Insh Marshes. A birchy knoll of fifty feet opens up the miles-wide world which is simply out of reach when you are down at water level. There are inevitable diversions: wolf-whistling wigeon flocks; a red squirrel on a birch trunk a dozen yards away, cramponing vertically upwards, three points of contact, one hind foot lifted to scratch some woodland irritant, hanging on; the whooper swans, of course, a handful swimming far out on dark pools, and one heart-stopper of a flypast – nine of them came low over the trees from behind me, then dropped almost to water level as they banked to fly south down the marshland miles. But such an hour, fasci-nating and sometimes enchanting as it was, reduced to five the workable, watchable daylight hours, and the particular old acquaintance I wished to meet had not shown up yet.

Realistically of course, you do not just drive a hundred pre-dawn miles, park your car at first light, walk down through the woods, focus your binoculars, and have the object of your day's endeavours manifest itself in the glasses, majestically lit by the rising sun, but you do try to harvest the fruits of the sum of your experience. You know what you are looking for and where you have seen it before. You know the kind of places it likes – low, solitary trees, fence posts. You fall back on proven techniques of stillness and moving through the landscape. If you don't like hides (I don't, although once in a while, needs must), you must become a part of the landscape. It all takes time. It all takes patience. That particular day, it would take two-and-a-half hours. Oh, and that was my third day of looking. It is, to say the least, an imperfect science. But after two-and-a-half hours, I focused my binoculars on a line of fence posts just beyond the edge of a long, narrow pool, and there on the third post from the left, in the sunlight, and perfectly reflected in the water, and exactly (down to the very fence post) where I had seen one two years ago, was a male hen harrier.

Apart from everything else that pushes the hen harrier so far up the list of bird conservation's priorities, it is a singularly stylish bird. Aesthetics alone would account for its superstar status in what you might call ornithology's pecking order. The male is the showstopper, and in light as uncompromising as a December noontide, and at a good distance, he looked white, and only a slightly darker white on his head and the tops of his folded wings, those wings which are ennobled by vivid black primaries. The legs looked bright yellow, and the face had a snowy-owlish aspect. No part of him moved. The male hen harrier is a master of stillness when he needs to be and he needs to be often because he is so conspicuous.

All stillness is a deception. It feigns disinterest. That particular manifestation of stillness in my binoculars was saying: don't bother about me, I'm a fence post. Such stillness also conceals the bird's true colours, metaphorically and literally, for the male hen harrier shares with the swans a quality in his plumage that absorbs colour from its surroundings. I stumbled on the phenomenon years ago when I was writing a book called *Waters of the Wild Swan* (Cape, 1992), in which I quoted the wildlife artist Charles Tunnicliffe. In his book *Bird Portraiture* (The Studio, 1946) he first dismissed the idea of a "white" bird, then there was this:

> *Notice the yellow tinge in the feathers of neck and upper breast, and the cold bluish purity of the back, wings and tail. Note also the colour of the shadowed under-surfaces and how it is influenced by the colour of the ground on which the bird is standing: if he is standing on green grass, then the underparts reflect a greenish colour, whereas if he were on dry, golden sand, the reflected colour would be of a distinctly warm tint; or again if he were flying over water, his breast, belly and underwings would take on a colder tint, especially if the water were reflecting a blue or a grey sky.*

But suppose the swan is swimming ahead of you, and straight into the sun:

> *... only his upper surfaces are lit by sunlight, the rest of him being in shadow and appearing dark violet against the bright*

water; in fact, but for the light on his back and the top of his head he appears as a dark silhouette in relation to the high tone of the water.

Snow changes everything:

Now you can see how yellow his neck is, and to a lesser extent, the rest of his upper plumage. Note also the reflected snow light on his undersides which makes them look almost the same tone as, or even lighter than, his top surfaces ...

The best wildlife artists are the best observers of wildlife (and most of them are also masters of stillness). If you want to see the full range of possibilities in the repertoire of that "white" hen harrier on the fence post, look up the archive of Donald Watson, who was – and remains a dozen years after his death – arguably the greatest observer of hen harriers, for he studied them throughout his life and he painted the results of his studies. One of the paintings that comes to mind shows a male bird flying very low over a snowy hillside in low mid-afternoon midwinter sunlight, and the bird is blue, for it has absorbed colour from both sky and snow (and the snow too has borrowed from the sky); and just as Tunnicliffe noted, the underside is lighter than the top surfaces.

It would be another hour before the Insh Marshes harrier flew, and what galvanised him was the arrival of the ringtail, the female harrier, a bird so different in plumage, so incon-spicuously brown that it looks like a different species, until, that is, you see them flying in tandem. And she brought with her a retinue of small birds, a cloud of finches, siskins and tits all twittering their displeasure and dicing with death to make their point. They looked like blown leaves in a November gale as they bowled across the marshes. For the next half hour the harriers came and went in and out of my vision, but they were rarely out of it for long and I judged that stillness would serve me best. Watching two harriers at work, hunting as a pair, demonstrating such mastery of the art of ultra-slow, low-level flight (only golden eagles do it better), tormenting the small birds of the marshes, striking down two within half an hour, sharing the meagre spoils, then taking to the air again, the ringtail like a mobile fragment of the winter landscape, the male a wizard of flickering colour change, while in the background, a pageant of the country's finest mountain massif drifts by in soft focus ... watching all that is to be transported to a more rarefied realm than the one I was occupying an hour ago.

It remains then, the grimmest of paradoxes that these birds are public enemy number one in the eyes of the grouse moor fraternity, that their beauty and their uncompromising and stylish wildness are of no account, simply because they are judged inconvenient for the most grotesque of all the human rituals Scotland has inflicted on its own landscape. The industry has grown tetchily defensive in response to mounting and sustained criticism of the toll it takes on Scotland's hen harrier population. Representatives of both landowners and gamekeepers have loudly and repeatedly condemned illegal killings, but they still happen, and the hen harrier remains an absentee from much of the landscape where it should thrive.

The longer the nights, the more precious the daylight.

Winter is the nadir for all our most vulnerable wildlife communities, the dark days for the weak and the ill-starred. Unless we find a new way to look after the land, we may be living through a hen harrier winter beyond which there is no second spring.

◉ ◉ ◉

Suddenly in early February, winter appeared to have found its voice. The mountain rescue teams were at work on Ben Nevis, on Mount Keen, and in the Garbh Choire of Bràigh Riabhach. One of the Cairngorms rescue team spoke of "full-on winter". On Mount Keen, the rescued climbers had been "woefully ill-prepared … it's winter folks, don't believe the hype". But there were only three weeks of meteorological winter left and the first daffodils were out, and some climbers had got careless because even in the mountains, winter had hardly bothered to show up. One of the main Highland ski centres hadn't opened until February. A week later I took advantage of an encouragingly wintry forecast and headed back to the Insh Marshes, hoping against hope for the bonus of a snowy day in Rothiemurchus or Abernethy.

I awoke in a Speyside hotel room at 3a.m. I opened the curtains on a sky stuffed with stars, the Cairngorms basking in moonlight and barely a shred of snow in sight. At 7a.m. there was ice on my car and fog shrouded the land. Talking to the hotel staff at breakfast, it turned out that full-on winter had lasted three days. I was at the Marshes by 8.30, the sun was making next to no impression on the fog. The descent from the footpath to the Invertromie hide was a carefully negotiated, ice-encrusted, frost-bound transition down through primeval-looking woodland. Sunlight had not penetrated down there for, oh, weeks probably. If it had not been for the all-pervasive pallor of the frost, the depth of shadow could have intimidated susceptible mortals. The hide itself is right down at marsh level and right in the outermost edge of the trees, a place on the cusp of two landscapes. At the door, it has a subterranean feeling. If you turn round, the wooded hillside you have just descended rears steeply above and shuts out all other sights and sounds of the overworld. The fact that it was bewitched by that ghostly off-white ermine of frost did not endear me to the job in hand.

Inside the hide, it seemed to be colder than outside, although that could just as easily have been a symptom of my aversion to hides. I discovered how much colder it was about to get when I opened the window slots that face out over the Marshes and a breeze drifted in bearing greetings from what's left of the Arctic sea ice. The window opened on a startling and panoramic sprawl of the Insh Marshes, the mountains beyond and the raw wildness of Strathspey at its most unfettered. The only problem was that I could see none of it because the fog had the place by the throat and appeared to have wrung the life out of it. Nothing moved. Nothing made a sound, at least nothing wild made a sound. The A9 made a sound, a distant and incongruous bass grumble, which at that moment in that situation was as a voice from another world. An hour frittered itself away into the blue-grey oblivion. My coffee flask, which was supposed to sustain me through elevenses and lunch, became my one defence against the nothingness of that hour. Then quite suddenly, and piece by piece, the nothing began to crack open, and a new Earth was born right in front of my eyes.

Mallards appeared, swimming. I have never been so pleased to see mallards, ever. Their pool appeared, then grew and grew until it became an acre of open water. I heard greylag goose voices (but saw no geese), a lapwing sighed (but I saw no lapwing). Then sunlight burst apart the mist to the north and revealed two roe deer a hundred yards apart between tall banks of reeds which dwarfed them. They looked grey in their winter garb, white scarves at their throats.

One pond after another, the intrinsic character of the Marshes began to reveal itself, and most ponds wore skins of ice. But the pace of the unveiling was surreally slow. It is in such situations that you realise how the idea of the slow-motion film was born. Then far above the Marshes a mountaintop appeared ... a mountaintop without a mountain to support it in the sky. It would take another half hour before the entire mountain had coloured itself in. It began to feel as if anything could happen.

Then one of the ponds loudly emptied itself of all its mallards, most of which I had not seen until that moment when twenty of them hurtled into the air, their flight unnaturally fast and their alarm cries unnaturally loud in the slow, soft context of the morning. Back on the water, something long and dark and blunt-nosed trailed a vee-shaped wake. It edged ashore, shook itself and stood in the sun watching the retreating, curving flight of the mallards. It was a big dog otter, and my guess was that it had been stalking the ducks and that the mist had cloaked its presence. I had never considered the possibility before of an otter using a ground mist to conceal itself as it hunted.

Sunlight had now reached to within about thirty yards of the hide, although the shadow of the hill behind would keep it from warming up the hide itself. Just beyond the edge of the shadow, a screen of reddish-looking scrubby birches was partially hiding another roe deer. It caught my eye only when it turned its back and the white blaze of its rump struck a jarring note, which blew its cover. It turned its head to look back along its spine and gave the hide a long, hard stare. I daresay the hide produced a lot of human noise from time to time, but this morning there had just been me, and making human noise is something I take pains to avoid when I'm alone in a situation like this. Then it stared hard left and its ears went forward. I looked where it was looking and there were two more roe deer, and these advanced soundlessly to where it stood, and for a moment all three had gathered in a tight bunch, the red of the birches in front of them and the sunlight full on them, and from their different angles they all turned their heads towards the hide, and presented me with one of my better roe deer photographs ("damned with faint praise" is the phrase you are looking for here). The smallest of the three, last year's young, was a markedly different shade of grey-brown from the others, a kind of olive shade. Olive, the other roe deer ...

For a long while they became the entire focus of my attention. It was clear they were feeding, but not at all clear what they were eating. The vegetation had that fag-end-of-winter look that promised no nutrition whatever, and the land where they stood was as much water and peaty mud as it was solid ground. Yet they fed constantly, but whatever they were eating was hidden from me by the long, pale, straw-coloured grass. Finally they emerged into a more open spot, and I realised how deep they were digging with forefeet and with muzzles, and that there was a great deal of tugging to free their food source. Roots. That's where there was new growth and nourishment, underground. It was turning into a surprising morning. I looked at my watch. It had been four hours.

I retraced my steps back up through the woods, the lower part of which was quite unaffected by sunlight. But as I climbed I could feel the air warm and the trees began to glitter and drip, hundreds of trees at a time, an extraordinary percussive symphony.

Back at the top of the wood, the sun suddenly poured through, and after my long shift in the frigid zone I stepped out into something that was properly warm. I guessed that the temperature had got a dozen degrees warmer in those few hundred uphill yards.

◉ ◉ ◉

It occurs to me as this exploration of winter advances that buzzards keep cropping up. There are good reasons why that should be so, not the least of which is their new-found abundance. One of the consequences of that is that many more people who are not instinctively drawn towards nature think they are seeing eagles, which brings the following conversation to mind.

So I met this man in a bar and he said:

"I know you. You're the nature guy."

I've been called worse. I nodded.

"Just saw a thing: it was a golden eagle sitting on a fence post."

And my head groaned inside itself and I thought, "Why me, God?" but I smiled instead and said:

"You sure? Buzzard, maybe?"

He shook his head.

"Eagle. It was huge."

And it was warm and comfortable in the bar and the fire was on and I had been reading the paper, so I really hadn't wanted conversation right then, right there, and I particularly didn't want the over-familiar buzzard-on-a-fence-post conversation. But I didn't want to appear rude either so I laid aside the paper, fixed the stranger with a tell-me-about-it kind of look and said:

"Tell me about it."

"Tell you what about it?"

"Where was your fence post?"

"At the side of the main road, a mile back."

"Now tell me what you saw."

His beer arrived. He drank the top third without pausing, sighed theatrically and nodded his appreciation.

"Long drive," he explained, then: "What did I see? It came up out of the grass verge as I drove past, almost hit the windscreen; carrying something furry in its legs – they were hanging down. And there was something white I couldn't see properly at first. But the road was empty so I pulled over on the verge and had a good look back. The furry thing had blood on it. It was under the eagle's feet."

Another swallow accounted for the second third of his pint. I said:

"Three things: one, did it perch upright or with its tail horizontal? Two, were its legs yellow or feathered? Three, was the white thing by any chance a plastic wing-tag?"

"Okay then. One, it perched upright. Two, the legs were bright yellow. Three, aye, it was a white disc stuck to one of the wings with a big ... "

"With a big letter C on it?"

"Aye. How'd you know?"

"Okay, you saw a buzzard, and a buzzard in your wind-screen IS huge!"

"Ach, is that all? I thought it was an eagle."

"Don't be disappointed. You saw an almost-eagle. A buzzard is a fabulous bird. After all, yours was impressive enough to make you think you'd seen an eagle. Don't think any less of it just because it wasn't what you thought, or wasn't what you wanted it to be. And that particular buzzard, with the white wing-tag with the big letter C on it, spends half its life walking about in the fields pretty much where you saw it, and most of the rest in the woods across the road."

"Why does it have the wing-tag? What's the C for?"

"Good questions. And I don't know, and I don't know anyone who does. I also don't know why anyone would want to tag a buzzard. But then I don't much care for wing-tagging birds at all. It's a device to satisfy the nosiness of people, and if you were to ask the bird, it would tell you it would rather not have wing-tags. No one has ever convinced me that the powers of flight of a bird with wing-tags are not hampered. The design of birds' wings has evolved for a few million years now and they've always used feathers. The addition of plastic makes a perfect design imperfect. And no one has ever convinced me that birds have not been killed when a tag snagged on a tree or a fence, or ..."

He hadn't bargained for this stuff and he had already lost interest. He downed the rest of his drink, announced his departure and his last words were these:

"Ah well, maybe you're right. I still think it was an eagle."

I mention the story because the buzzard must be the most misidentified bird in the Highlands, especially among people who are new to the Highlands or very occasional visitors and the one thing they want to see before they leave is a golden eagle, and the notion must have come into my mind at least partly because I was back in the Insh Marshes, and there are few better places in the land to put the two species into some kind of perspective. My simple rule of thumb is this: if you are in any doubt, it's not a golden eagle. But that is of limited use to someone who is in no doubt at all because they don't know what an eagle looks like in relation to a buzzard, or what a buzzard looks like in relation to an eagle. You can refine that idea by considering the bird's environment. You don't get golden eagles sitting at the side of the B970, so the chances are that if you see something eagle-shaped and magnified by an early morning fog sitting on a telegraph pole at the roadside and watching you as you drive slowly past, with the best will in the world that's not a golden eagle, that's a buzzard. On the other hand, you don't get buzzards at 5,000 feet and still climbing. So if you see what looks like a small golden eagle high overhead when you're on the Cairngorms plateau and you think it's small enough to be a buzzard, it's just that the scale of the place has defeated your eyes and it's an eagle a thousand feet higher and still climbing. And on yet another hand, the Insh Marshes some 3,000 feet lower than the plateau, and a landscape flat enough to command the River Spey to dawdle in the western lee of the Cairngorms for a few miles ... that is buzzard territory *par excellence*, and buzzard territory *par excellence* sometimes produces extraordinary results.

When I am not refrigerating myself in one of the RSPB's hides at the Marshes, my favourite viewpoint there is a blunt headland of heather and rock and birch trees. It shoulders out from the mountain massif to invade the edge of the Marshes, a low outpost with miles-wide views. I go often in autumn, winter and earliest spring, mostly to prospect for whooper swans, but also for all the swans' fellow travellers that find reason to linger there, and for the place itself, for its hard-nosed mountain landscape setting. The word "landscape" is slightly misleading, for mostly, and especially in winter, it's more water than land, and it's that combination of shallow water lying over grass that endears it to the swans, to all wildfowl and to the nature writer. There was a day when I washed up there a few winters ago and the swans were half a mile away and scattered widely, and I wouldn't be able get any closer to them without getting back into the car and driving all the way round, and I was done with driving for the moment. I filed the idea away as a possibility for the end of the day if they were still there, but as it was, there were geese and lapwings in a field of grudgingly rough grazing on the very mountain edge of the marshes. The sharp, querulous staccatos of the greylags were shrapnel for the ears, flung by a north wind with an unforgiving edge, whereas the thin, woozy sighs of the lapwings rather drifted up on it, a sound that bathed the landscape like a gentle wave of newly melted ice. Yet there was a satisfyingly yin-yang-ish harmonious aspect to the resulting blend, which somehow amounted to rather more than the sum of its parts.

Enter from directly overhead that old familiar contralto downcurve, that bluesy minor-third, that haunted voice, and I leaned back and looked up to forage among the purple tracery of winter birch branches until, in a clear patch of cold blue, I found the thickly patterned spreadeagle of buzzard wings. The bird was moving sideways into the wind as if it were being towed along by the primary feathers of its starboard wing. For all my determined stillness, I was being watched, assessed, dismissed, and the bird cruised on towards the lapwing field, still going sideways ...and followed at once by its own mirror image crossing the same patch of sky, and it too was flying sideways against the wind but leading with the port wing. Because I was looking at the underside of the second bird's wings from below and behind, as opposed to below and in front with the first bird, I saw their rich patterns in a quite different light. And the patterns themselves differed from bird to bird, because, as I have suggested elsewhere, there is no standard buzzard uniform.

So there were two birds out over the lapwing-and-goose field, and for a moment it had seemed like a good idea to change position so that I had a view of the field and its airspace unencumbered by branches. Memo to self – don't. At least not yet. I have found that when you are in buzzard country *par excellence*, there are often more pairs of buzzard eyes watching you than you know about, which is why I have developed this slightly odd-looking technique (I'm guessing here, I've never watched myself) of standing with my back against a birch trunk, and slowly inching all the way round the tree looking up and keeping my back in contact with the trunk. Although I knew there were two buzzards out there to the north, which was the direction I was facing, and although I also knew that two buzzards over a field full of lapwings and geese can sometimes put on quite a show if they're in the mood, I began my slow circumnavigation of the birch by turning away from the buzzards and towards the east.

I was a degree or two beyond east-north-east when the third and then the fourth buzzards cruised over the trees, one looking down at me looking up, the other looking side-headed at the sky. The third called from no more than thirty feet up and directly overhead, a cry so sharp-edged and (as I fancied it) so specifically aimed that I felt it nail me to the tree. Tingling scalp and startled shoulder blades jerked back against the bark in a tiny but perfectly co-ordinated spasm of response. It was an ice-cold voice the bird directed straight at me.

It is absurd, of course. The buzzard and I both know I don't speak buzzard. It was calling the attention of the fourth buzzard to my presence. And I had been so convinced I would be indistinguishable from the birch trunk where I leaned to any third and fourth buzzard eyes, thanks to my inch-perfect, slow-motion manoeuvre around the trunk. The fourth buzzard called back and immediately appeared in that portion of the sky where the third still lingered. The two birds shared that space for a moment and called there just once, but the call of the fourth bird began just before the call of the third bird, so that their voices overlapped, and as one was more or less a tone above the other and curved in a steeper glissando arc to a deeper denouement, the effect was of a kind of menacing harmony unique in all my days and nights in wild places. I imagined a duet of wolfsong dwindling to its last deepening and discordant bars.

The two buzzards veered towards the north as the first two had done, flying sideways, the starboard wingtip of one almost touching the port wingtip of the other, so that it was a single creature with a double wingspan that crossed the clear sky directly overhead, and I thought that if the thirsty traveller in the bar had seen this, he would have held the almost-eagle in formidable respect forever more, for I have done just that myself.

It was time to give up trying to be a birch tree, time to walk slowly to that space on the headland where the trees relented and offered up a wide view over the lapwings' field. The original buzzards were still there, circling at more or less my eye level and about a hundred yards away, and so were buzzards five and six; and buzzards three and four cruised over the birches that surrounded me on three sides, and now the buzzards had become a throng. Six buzzards at eye-level and in the sunlight, and loitering without any apparent intent at all, but – also apparently – enjoying the company of the others less than a month before the nesting season begins with all guns blazing, all hackles raised ... it was a moment to weigh up every ounce of that compact, power-packed profile, to garner tiny flight details for future use (one bird paused on stiffly held wings to lift a foot towards its beak and nibble it for several seconds; one half-folded its wings and surged forward in level flight as if a turbocharger had just kicked in; one hovered on slowly beating wings, tail held vertically below its head). And then, from behind and above, the seventh buzzard called, and then from the low ground beyond the geese, I heard another, so I turned and re-focussed the glasses, and through a blur of mobilising greylag geese there were three more buzzards, and these abandoned what had been a leisurely northwards procession and made a pointed beeline for the throng.

Ten buzzards.

So let's see. I had come here to watch the swans, but I had come here too knowing the place from old seasons and its capacity to surprise me with its wildlife riches. I had come to this side of the headland in the first place because I had heard geese, then their lapwing companions, and decided I would drop in on their field to see what was unfolding there. Then, buzzard by buzzard, the whole mood of the hour transformed, and when the last three panicked the goose hordes, the sky was as full of big beating wings as any single pair of human eyes could possibly take in. And then I felt as if – finally – I had achieved something of the birch's stillness, for I was still and the sky seethed and the air resounded with the clatter of several hundred geese and the eerie tumult of ten buzzard voices that wheeled and dived and soared and spiralled as they cried and … hey, what happened to the lapwings?

There is a school of thought, to be found exclusively in the minds of a section of the country's gamekeepers, that there are too many buzzards, and that it should be made easier to get a licence to shoot them. This is why, because sometimes buzzards turn up ten at a time, because their range is spreading, because they constitute that rarest phenomenon in the 21st-century landscape of Scotland, a prospering species of raptor. It is almost unheard of in our recent past, thanks in no small measure to the activities of that certain section of gamekeepers. Two things have happened to assist the buzzards' cause. One is that pro-wildlife legislation has got tougher and is better policed, and the other is wildlife crimes are much more widely publicised in the media. So those keepers who cannot tolerate the improving fortunes of a wild creature if it causes them the slightest inconvenience have raised the cry again with Scottish Government ministers:

"Too many buzzards!"

But there is no such thing. There can be no such thing. It is one of the most basic principles of nature that an abundance of predators is only possible when there is a superabundance of prey, and if that prey includes literally millions of gamekeepers' pheasants that are released into our countryside every year, it also includes rabbits, rats, voles, stoats and weasels, and various other forms of what they are pleased to call vermin.

Not all keepers feel this way. I have had invigorating conversations with those who like to work with nature rather than against it; who know that when the population of a raptor like a buzzard soars from a troubling low point to a spectacular high, that high is false and soon enough the population will relax back to a stable level. Besides, you don't remove protection from a protected species just because it has recently achieved a position of strength. But all that presupposes that no one takes the law into their own hands;

the landscape *is* still pockmarked with poisoned carcases. Strange how public opinion never comes down on the side of the poisoners.

Hopefully this time the buzzard is here to stay.

Rejoice.

And no one should worry that it's not an eagle.

ALMOST EAGLE

Buzzard is almost eagle,
more than hawk,
opens tins of cold air
with cutting edges
of sunwise spirals.
Blue's the background sky
best suited to such languid copper,
not golden enough for eagle
which prefers thundercloud grey.

Chapter Fourteen

I Went Out to the Hazel Wood

THEY CLING TO THE outermost edges of the western fringes of Gaeldom like the frayed hem of an ancient kilt. They are rags and tatters of woodland, remnants of remnants. They are among the last souvenirs of the original wildwood, the most primitive and least tampered-with of its direct ancestors. The Atlantic hazel woods of our western seaboard – and a handful more on Ireland's west coast – constitute a habitat unique in the world. Perhaps they are the oldest of all the native habitats of post-Ice-Age Scotland. They hold the great ice in their memory, and in their DNA. Perhaps they have something to say to me about the nature of what winter has become. It is a nature writer's mission rather than a climatologist's, but then this book, this tetralogy of the seasons, is a nature writer's mission. I advocate listening to the land, and I practise what I advocate. Winter has become so unstable, so unsure of itself, so erratic; winter has lost its sense of purpose; winter has lost its way; winter is just plain lost. I have emerged from this pilgrimage through winter looking for something stable and eternal to cling to myself. And nothing clings to eternity more tenaciously than an Atlantic hazel wood.

From the west coasts of Sutherland and Ross to Skye to Ardnamurchan to Mull to Knapdale and the island of Seil in Argyll, these dense and low-slung woods curve uphill from the ocean's high-tide line to a distinctive pattern dictated by the wind. They will never grow taller, and for as long as they have held the final frontier of the land against the onslaught of ocean winds, they never have. The ocean has never overwhelmed them but ocean winds limit them. Tree and ocean have reached an amicable pact, a peace treaty that has lasted 10,000 years.

Step inside such a wood, on the west coast of Mull. Feel the millennia tumble away. Immerse yourself in its embrace and the press of trees abruptly reduces your awareness of the world to the next few yards, sometimes the next few feet. Again and again the architecture of such a wood commands you to turn aside, bend double, unpin yourself from brambles, wade bogs … any combination of these and more or less all the time.

And the trees are eerie.

They writhe their trunks and limbs, the ones that have trunks and limbs, that is. Many of them are effectively self-coppicing, that is, they produce dozens of stems instead of a single trunk. Our own distant ancestors learned from nature how to coppice trees, and especially hazels, so that they might create endless supplies of firewood and of straight poles for building. Often in the Atlantic hazel woods, the trees just do it themselves. If you walk there in a certain mindset and if the day is soft grey and calm, the effect can seem curiously aggressive, nervy, edgy; and if the sun shines, they throw such a web of shadows on the woodland floor that it adds to the untranquil aura of such places. When Yeats went out to the hazel wood in *The Song of Wandering Aengus* "because a fire was in my head", it was not to cool the fire that he went there, but rather to cut a hazel wand so that he might catch a trout. The uneasiness of hazel woods is not the environment you would choose to cool a fiery head. If, on the other hand, what you want is an instant fishing rod, it's perfect.

Hazel woods are also vocal. The trees rasp and rustle in a good-going wind (and on Scotland's Atlantic seaboard the wind is good-going more often than not), and groan and creak when the wind gets excited, and these are notes of protest that ocean winds have heard for almost as long as there have been hazel woods on an Atlantic shore.

Everything here is apparently ageless, or at least it evokes those imponderable times ensnared within the implicit vagueness of the word "Mesolithic". It means, since you asked, relating to a transitional period of the Stone Age between the Palaeolithic and the Neolithic, so somewhere between 12000 and 3000 BC. Further back than that, we're guessing beyond the level of our competence, but there is ample evidence to suggest that at least some of our Mesolithic ancestors knew how to burn and cut, both to improve grass for the animals they hunted and to create more prolific hazel woods that produced more wood for building, more firewood and more nuts. The profusion of hazelnut shells unearthed by archaeologists at some of our oldest known human settlements is emphatic confirmation of their importance as a food source and, crucially, a food source that could be harvested and stored for winter. For such people, hazelnuts *were* the nature of winter.

It occurred to me too, walking this Mull wood, that prob-ably then as now, hazel woods were also a preferred habitat of brambles, and that too would enhance their value to early wanderers and settlers. And the more inclined to settle our ancestors became, the more valuable were their hazel woods. The mysterious crannog builders, for example, used hazel and alder posts, and both are trees that thrive in wetlands. The earliest farmers in the West Highlands laid claim to hazel thickets or planted their own, and found endless uses for the flexible slim branches: Yeats's Wandering Aengus was not the first man who ever caught a little silver trout by hooking a berry to a thread on the end of a hazel wand. They also make good fences, creels, any shape or size of basket you care to imagine, hoops for barrels. There were creel houses and outbuildings like barns made from hazel. In a daft moment, I wondered how I would begin to make a creel house if I had been a wandering Mesolithic chiel 5,000 years ago and made landfall hereabouts. I decided I would make two circles first, a small one which would let the smoke out from a central fire, and a large one that would define the floor area, and which could be pinned into the ground like a tent. Then all you have to do is join the two together with curving hazel wands to make a dome, then cross-hatch them with hori-zontal hazel wands. Nature has always approved of its tribes – and we are one of these, remember – living in something so organic, something so characteristic of the landscape where it stands. And sometimes, when we do still take the time and the trouble to listen to nature, we surprise ourselves. In some parts of England, for example, where hazels can reach fifty feet high (they achieve nowhere near half that on this blasted shore), they are conservationists. They are being planted and coppiced beneath oak trees right now to assist the cause of English bluebells and nightingales, and who would not want to assist the cause of both?

Meanwhile, on Mull at the end of a weary winter, it seems they assist the cause of brown hares. I walked in on two of them resting in dappled sunlight, ears flat along their backs, both reluctant to move despite my blundering intrusion. When eventually they lost their nerve and decided to make a run for it, they effected a half-hearted retreat across the woodland floor and stopped again not twenty yards away, and still well inside the trees, sitting up and looking back, ears tall. It seemed to my eyes that a hazel wood was a confining kind of habitat for a hare, but then I wondered if perhaps it was an extra defensive measure these hares had adopted in recognition of Mull's steadily growing population of sea eagles. This coast in particular is increasingly accustomed to that huge eagle shadow rippling across shoreline and cliff face; across its hazel woods. I pulled back, chose a different route, stopped out of sight and downwind and waited. In ten minutes, the hares had ambled back to the very glade where I had found them.

The moment put in mind an old September in this very wood, the shoreline air thick with young swallows and martins cashing in on the insect hordes above and around the hazel wood. I had one eye on a bruise-coloured storm that was powering its way across the sea towards this Mull shore from Tiree and Coll, both of which had vanished in the last few minutes. I heard it coming, for it packed its own wind and arrived with a salvo of hailstones that sizzled off the sea, off the shoreline rocks, then off the trees. By that time, the swallows, the martins and I had come to the same snap decision – head for the hazel wood. I had stepped into the lee of one of the bulkier non-hazels of the wood, a silver birch, and almost at once the skinniest twigs of the surrounding hazels were invaded by birds. They perched upright, chattering, dozens of them in a few square yards. I had seen this happen before in reed beds, but not in a wood. There again, a hazel wood a yard above the high-tide line probably doesn't look so different from a reed bed, when all you want to do is get your head down in a storm, when your solitary need is met by something thin and upright to cling to.

The storm crashed by, the sun rushed out, and the birds, as if on a signal, exploded in a whispered cacophony of rasping wings back up into the insect-rich air and resumed the slaughter. One moment there were swallows and martins all around as thick on the hazel trees as catkins in February. The next, there were only leaves for company, and in the stillness that followed the storm's gusto, the trees' voices were the whispers of skeletons couched in an antique tongue.

It is curious how some landscapes draw you in and reach you with at least a sense of their formative years. Some achieve the trick by baring the rock bones of the landscape corpus. Some – glaciers or the aftermath of glaciers, for example – demonstrate at a glance the convulsive nature of the hand that devised the architecture of their landscape. Others – like volcanoes, like sea, like polar ice – use perpetual restlessness to challenge our own transience. A Scots pine wood uses the deep, dark green primitiveness of jungles, a realm so all-consuming that you cannot imagine that the landscape ever wore any other garb. They have in common with the hazel woods that they trace their ancestors directly back to the great ice, and they contemplated no other guise from that day to this. Such a pedigree communicates itself effortlessly.

But an Atlantic hazel wood has a different technique from any of these. It lies along the westmost edge of the land as if it has just waded ashore, or as if a mighty breaking wave had petrified as it unfurled, then fossilised over millennia into a chaotic tsunami of trees. I know, I know, I'm taking liberties with the evolution of the raw stuff of the planet, but these are trees unlike any other. If your idea of the kind of tree that makes you happy is a trunk from which branches and a canopy spring forth, you are in the wrong wood here. Rather, this is a half-caste wood, biologically rooted between a tree and a shrub. From inland and above, or from the sea homing in on the land, the thing looks neat, ordered, corralled and curved by the ocean and its winds into something compliant and obedient. But inside, it seethes. There is a crackling, spindly, electric energy about a tree with thirty trunks, each of which rocks and swithers independently of all the rest and at the wind's bidding; each of which throws a shadow on the woodland floor. And every dancing shadow is interlaced with the dancing shadows of the next tree and the next, for it is in the nature of hazels in an Atlantic wood not to leave more space between trees than what is strictly necessary to get the job done. The whole thing has the effect of a dance to the music of time.

So might it then have been a woodland like this one, but on Skye rather than Mull, that determined the outcome of an epic fight between the Ulster hero Cuchullin and the Skye warrior-goddess Skiach, for it was known even then (and whenever "then" may have been) that hazelnuts possessed a magic that conferred knowledge on those who ate them? One of many versions of the legend has it that when Cuchullin heard that Skiach was operating a school for heroes in the Cuillin of Skye, he crossed the sea in three strides to land at Talisker Bay, for he was already a true hero and he was intent on wiping out the opposition. Skiach enrolled him in her school and he proceeded to defeat every pupil in hand-to-hand combat. This impressed Skiach enough to permit him to fight her daughter, whom he also defeated. This in turn infuriated Skiach to the extent that she deigned to descend from the mountains to fight Cuchullin herself. They fought inconclusively for days, until finally Skiach's daughter persuaded them to pause long enough to eat a deer roast that had been stuffed with hazelnuts. The two combatants reckoned privately that the hazel wisdom would give them the knowledge to defeat the other. Instead, it gave them the knowledge to realise that neither could overcome the other, so they made peace instead. They also made this pact: that if either should ever need the assistance of the other, it would be given unconditionally "though the sky fall and crush us". Cuchullin returned to Ulster. Skiach called the mountains after him – Cuillin.

It is more than just a wood you enter when you step into the edgy embrace of an Atlantic hazel wood, more than just food you acquire when you eat the nuts of an Atlantic hazel, and it was ever thus. The legend imitates nature, imitates the pact the hazel wood made with the ocean, that both might thrive and accommodate each other.

The thing is, it works. At the end of a winter in which the dominant characteristic was a climate in chaos, a chaos contrived by our confrontation with nature, the moral of the story was never more obvious. We are Cuchullin and Skiach before they ate the hazelnuts; if we are to pull back from an abyss of unknown depths and disasters, we have to stop the fight. It can be done, a way can be found, we can be the hazel wood to nature's ocean.

Nature tells us that every day. But first, we need to take heed. We need to listen.

Acknowledgements

I SEE FROM THE Acknowledgements in this book's predecessor, *The Nature of Autumn,* that "I edge closer to poets and artists with the passage of time." It seems the process only deepens.

I doff my cap to William Butler Yeats again in these pages.

And my late great friend George Garson is here again too, and he was both artist and poet. It is probably time that I stopped trying to grapple with the nature of the debt that I owe him, and just be grateful that our paths crossed and that as a result my life was – and continues to be – immeasurably enriched.

For a Scottish nature writer working primarily in Scotland, the process has occasionally immersed me in the works of others furth of Scotland, some of them considerably furth. Shingi Itoh may not be a name on the lips of many readers and writers of nature books, but his book, *The White Egret,* is a masterclass in the art of nature photography. I have known and loved it for thirty years and finally I have the opportunity to pay it due tribute, now that little egrets have begun to creep into the fiefdom where I ply my trade.

I have long been grateful to the painter Charles Tunnicliffe for his thoughtful reading of the plumage of swans, and although it was doubtless intended in the first place as a kind of memo to himself, it is an object lesson for me in how the seeing eye of the artist is one of the most prized assets a nature writer can add to his toolbox.

And a couple of generations down the line, a young Fife-based painter (and incidentally a singularly entertaining blogger) called Leo Du Feu is one to watch. We've worked together at book festivals, and in the context of this book we went whale-watching on the Forth. He has that virtue that George Garson used to extol: "Control, but relaxed control, mind."

Other writers, of course, continue to cast their spell, and none is more enduring and more important to the kind of nature writer I have become than Seton Gordon. He is one of my orginal sources. And it was Gavin Maxwell who first made me aware of the possibilities of writing about the land for a living.

Aldo Leopold's *A Sand County Almanac* (written in 1940s Wisconsin) remains unopposed in my mind as the very pinnacle of the art of nature writing. My Alaskan friend Nancy Lord is one of Leopold's heirs, a powerful writer who is also increasingly involved in teaching the troubling science of climatology. And Roger Payne, an American whale biolo-gist, wrote in *Among Whales* the finest work on the subject I know.

Thank you all, the living and the no longer living, for the benevolent influences of your work on this Scottish nature writer.

Finally, the most heartfelt vote of thanks of all is for my publisher Sara Hunt of Saraband, her editor Craig Hillsley, and my literary agent Jenny Brown. They are a kind of dream team for my kind of writer.

The
Nature of
Autumn

A pilgrimage through the shapes and shades of autumn

In autumn nature stages some of its most enchantingly beautiful displays; yet it's also a period for reflection – melancholy, even – as the days shorten and winter's chill approaches.

Charting the colourful progression from September through October and November, Jim Crumley tells the story of how unfolding autumn affects the wildlife and landscapes of his beloved countryside. Along the way, Jim experiences the deer rut, finds phenomenal redwood trees in the most unexpected of places, and contemplates climate change, the death of his father, and his own love of nature.

He paints an intimate and deeply personal portrait of a moody and majestic season.

Longlisted for the Wainwright Golden Beer Prize